T0022149

POCKET **ROUGH GUIDE**

ITALIAN LAKES

WALKS & TOURS

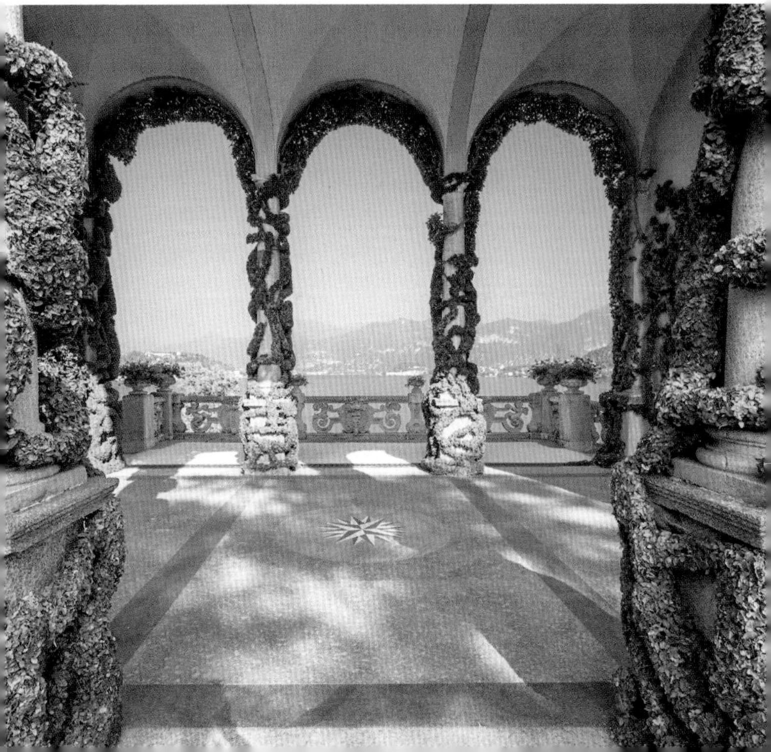

YOUR TAILOR-MADE TRI

STARTS HERE

Tailor-made trips and unique adventures crafted by local expert

Rough Guides has been inspiring travellers with lively and thought-provoking guidebooks for more than 35 years. Now we're linking you up with selected local experts to craft your dream trip. They will put together your perfect itinerary and book it at local rates.

Don't follow the crowd – find your own path.

HOW ROUGHGUIDES.COM/TRIPS WORKS

STEP 1

Pick your dream destination, tell us what you want and submit an enquiry.

STEP 2

Fill in a short form to tell your local expert about your dream trip and preferences.

STEP 3

Our local expert will craft your tailor-made itinerary. You'll be able to tweak and refine it until you're completely satisfied.

STEP 4

Book online with ease, pack your bags and enjoy the trip! Our local expert will be on hand 24/7 while you're on the road.

BENEFITS OF PLANNING AND BOOKING AT ROUGHGUIDES.COM/TRIPS

PLAN YOUR ADVENTURE WITH LOCAL EXPERTS

Rough Guides' English-speaking local experts are hand-picked, based on their experience in the travel industry and their impeccable standards of customer service.

SAVE TIME AND GET ACCESS TO LOCAL KNOWLEDGE

When a local expert plans your trip, you save time and money when you book, even during high season. You won't be charged for using a credit card either.

MAKE TRAVEL A BREEZE: BOOK WITH PEACE OF MIND

Enjoy stress-free travel when you use Rough Guides' secure online booking platform. All bookings come with a money-back guarantee.

WHAT DO OTHER TRAVELLERS THINK ABOUT ROUGH GUIDES TRIPS?

Trip to Spain

This Spain tour company did a fantastic job to make our dream trip perfect. We gave them our travel budget, told them where we would like to go, and they did all of the planning. Our drivers and tour guides were always on time and very knowledgable. The hotel accommodations were better than we would have found on our own. Only one time did we end up in a location that we had not intended to be in. We called the 24 hour phone number, and they immediately fixed the situation.

Don A, USA ★★★★★

Trip to Morocco

Our trip was fantastic! Transportation, accommodations, guides – all were well chosen! The hotels were well situated, well appointed and had helpful, friendly staff. All of the guides we had were very knowledgeable, patient, and flexible with our varied interests in the different sites. We particularly enjoyed the side trip to Tangier! Well done! The itinerary you arranged for us allowed maximum coverage of the country with time in each city for seeing the important places.

Sharon, USA ★★★★★

PLAN AND BOOK YOUR TRIP AT
ROUGHGUIDES.COM/TRIPS

CONTENTS

Introduction

Best Walks & Tours for... **6**
Discover the Italian Lakes **10**
Food and drink **16**
Shopping **20**
Entertainment **22**
Activities **24**
Chronology **26**

Best itineraries

Tour 1: The Borromean Islands **30**
Tour 2: Stresa and Angera Castle **34**
Tour 3: Monte Mottarone and Santa Caterina **38**
Tour 4: Villa Taranto and Lake Mergozzo **40**
Tour 5: Lake Maggiore Express **44**
Tour 6: Lake Orta **48**
Tour 7: Varese and Lake Lugano **52**
Tour 8: Villa Carlotta and Bellagio **56**
Walk 9: Como Town and Brunate cable-car **60**
Tour 10: Ramo di Como and Villa del Balbianello **64**
Walk 11: Bergamo **70**
Tour 12: Lake Iseo **74**
Tour 13: The Franciacorta wine trail **79**
Walk 14: Sirmione **82**
Tour 15: Lake Garda cruise **86**
Tour 16: Gardone Riviera **90**
Tour 17: A taste of Trentino **94**
Walk 18: Milan **98**

Directory

Accommodation **104**
Restaurants **114**
Essentials **124**
Language **134**
Books and Film **136**
About This Book **138**
Credits **139**
Index **140**

Art lovers

View rich collections of Renaissance art, from Bergamo's Accademia Carrara (walk 11) to Milan's Museo Poldi Pezzoli and Pinacoteca di Brera, home to Leonardo da Vinci's *The Last Supper* (walk 18).

Best Walks & Tours for...

Castle enthusiasts

Lake Garda's shores (walk 14 and tour 15) are studded with medieval castles. Trentino (tour 17) is dotted with fortifications, while Angera (tour 2) is home to the imposing Rocca Borromeo.

Escaping the crowds

Take a dip in unspoilt Lake Mergozzo where boats with engines are banned (tour 4), or spend time on the tranquil shores of Lake Iseo (tour 12). Relatively unexplored Franciacorta (tour 13) is a pretty region for touring and wine tasting.

Ferry trips

Sit back and let the ferries do the work for you. The cruises from Stresa to Locarno (tour 5), Como to Bellagio (tour 10) and Sirmione to Malcesine (tour 15) are among the most scenic.

Food and wine

Vinophiles and gourmets will enjoy Franciacorta (tour 13), home of Italy's finest sparkling wine and many great restaurants. Bergamo (walk 11) is a foodie favourite. The culinary scene in Milan (walk 18) caters for all tastes.

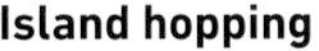

Island hopping

Follow the crowds to the Borromean Islands (tour 1); visit Lake Orta's Isola di San Giulio (tour 6). Hike or bike around Lake Iseo's Monte Isola (tour 12).

Shopping

Head to the factory outlets of Como (walk 9), for discounted designer clothes and accessories; or browse in the boutiques of Bellagio (tour 8) or Bergamo (walk 11).

Villas and gardens

Lake Maggiore's showpiece is Villa Taranto (tour 4), while Lake Como boasts villas Carlotta, Melzi and Serbelloni (tour 8) and the movie regular Villa del Balbianello (tour 10).

INTRODUCTION

An introduction to the Italian Lakes and what makes it special, what not to miss and what to do when you're there.

Discover the Italian Lakes 10
Food and drink 16
Shopping 20
Entertainment 22
Activities 24
Chronology 26

Discover the Italian Lakes

With a mild climate, romantic waterfront views and lush vegetation, the lakes have long been a favoured haunt. Add sports, culture, fashion and gastronomy, and it is little wonder that they remain one of Italy's most popular tourist hotspots.

The deep glacial lakes of northern Italy lie between the southern foothills of the Alps, near the Swiss border, and the low-lying plains of the Po Valley. The famous trio are Lake Como, which lies north of the great metropolis of Milan, Lake Maggiore to the city's northwest and Lake Garda to the east. Although the lakes extend over four regions – Piedmont, Lombardy, Trentino and Veneto – the area is comparatively small and easily covered by car or public transport. The A4 autostrada provides a quick way of getting across the region, and for those who want to explore the shopping delights of Milan, the city is no more than an hour away from Stresa or Como by car or train.

Shaping the lakes

It was glaciers at the end of the last Ice Age that gouged out the ribbons of water that are now the lakes. For over 10,000 years inhabitants have also left their mark on the region, from the prehistoric rock engravings in the Camonica Valley to the remains of Roman villas to the castles and *palazzi* of the ruling dynasties. The Lombard plain was hardly ideal terrain on which to settle: the marshes needed to be drained and the water channelled into canals. Yet by medieval times it was domesticated and dotted with castles, churches, abbeys and palaces. The transformation, from bog to economic powerhouse, was thanks largely to the industriousness of the lakeside towns' natives and the advent of a prosperous local mercantile class.

Local culture

The lakes region's complex culture can be divided into discrete mini-cultures. The four different regions of the lakes area all have clearly separate identities. But it is the bond with, and loyalty to, their home town that many Italians feel most deeply. The Comaschi (natives of Como), for example, live in close proximity to Milan, one of Europe's great cities, and yet, far from embracing the cosmopolitan life of the city, they identify only with their own town. Members of Como's old commercial families have known each other since infancy and do business together in a relaxed way. The strong sense of regional identity is also reflected in the host of different

Twilight over Bellagio, Lake Como

dialects and – of more interest to travellers – cuisines within the region.

Visitors to the lakes

The lakes have long cast a spell over visitors. The Romans were enamoured of the lakeside spas – Catullus owned a villa at Sirmione and Pliny the Younger built two villas at Bellagio. Travellers on the Grand Tour, after a treacherous journey over the Alps, were awestruck by the sudden vision of the sublime lakes and the Mediterranean flora that flourished on the shores. Shelley, Wordsworth and other Romantic poets were bewitched by the dramatic natural beauty of the deep-blue waters and mountain peaks. Henry James was almost, but not quite, lost for words:

'On, on into Italy we went – a rapturous progress through a wild luxuriance of corn and olives and figs and mulberries and chestnuts and frescoed villages and clamorous beggars and all the good old Italianisms of tradition.' The sight of sluggish steamers and snow-clad peaks still stirs visitors. But as James said of Lake Como, 'It's the place to enjoy *à deux* – it's a shame to be here in gross melancholy solitude.'

Rich, royal and famous

By the late 19th century, the lakes had become a pleasure ground for the rich, royal and famous. In 1879 Queen Victoria stayed at **Villa Clara at Baveno** on Lake Maggiore. In the same decade, Lake Garda – notably the resort of Arco in Trentino – became a retreat for Austrian grand-dukes. While the aristocracy of Mitteleuropa flocked to the sanatoria around Lake Garda, the lake was also appreciated by writers and politicians: the **Grand Hotel** in **Gardone Riviera** was patronised

A long life in Limone

The citizens of Limone sul Garda on the northwest shore of Lake Garda have one of the highest rates of life expectancy in Europe, with a large number of healthy residents over eighty. The absence of heart disease here has been studied by many scientists, who variously ascribe this exceptional healthiness to climate, diet or genes. The village was isolated until the 1930s – only accessible by boat or by crossing the mountains – so the secret may lie in a limited gene pool and rare blood group. A mystery protein in the locals' blood, known as Apolipoprotein A-1 (or Apo A-1 Milano), appears to purge fat from the arteries and give a much-reduced susceptibility to heart attacks and strokes. All the carriers are descendants of a couple who married in 1644. Genes aside, a mild climate, stress-free lifestyle and cholesterol-free diet of lemons, lake fish and olives all contribute to the fine health of Lake Garda's residents.

The picturesque village of Bardolino on Lake Garda

Don't leave the Italian Lakes without...

Getting wet. Take a towel and head down to the lake for a swim. Choose from hundreds of kilometres of shoreline and many different lakes. Tiny Lago di Mergozzo is the cleanest of them all. See page 43.

Rewarding yourself with an ice cream. Discover the delicious delights of Italian ice cream at a local gelateria. See page 37.

Indulging in wine tasting. Experience the local wine culture by visiting vineyards and wineries around the Italian lakes, where you can sample exquisite wines produced in the region's fertile hills and valleys. See page 22.

Partaking in *aperitivo* hour. The after-work happy-hour *aperitivo* has become very much a way of life across much of Italy, and especially around Milan. Stylish bars and cafés serve a sensational range of cocktails, with *stuzzichini* (snacks) and elegant canapés. See page 99.

Sightseeing by boat. Arguably the best way to appreciate the glorious scenery around the lakes is from in the middle of them. Choose from fast or slow options, with the possibility at hopping on and off en route. See page 130.

Reaching the dizzy heights. Take the pain out of climbing the mountains of the lakes by taking a cable-car (funicular). All you have to do is enjoy the views as you go up. See pages 63 and 89.

Sampling some fish from the lakes. So fresh it's almost still flapping, lake fish can be tried as an antipasto, in risottos and pasta, and, as a secondo, perhaps simply grilled, baked or fried. See page 81.

Learning about silk. The manufacture of silks, velvets, brocades and damasks began in Como in the 16th century. Although silkworms are no longer bred around the lake, Chinese thread is woven and dyed here to the exact specifications of leading Milanese fashion houses. On the outskirts of the city is the **Museo Didattico della Seta** (Museum of Silk; Via Castelnuovo 9; www.museosetacomo.com; charge), which documents the story of Como's silk. See page 21.

by Vladimir Nabokov and Somerset Maugham, and it became Winston Churchill's base for painting holidays.

Celebrity status

Today the lakes provide a weekend or holiday retreat for Milanese industrialists, Russian tycoons and a handful of fashion designers and celebrities. The 'Clooney Effect' (George has a 25-room villa at Laglio) has sent property prices rocketing on the southern shores of Lake Como. The **Villa del Balbianello**, also on Lake Como, has acquired celebrity status by

Vineyard in Franciacorta

featuring in a number of blockbuster movies (see page 137). The lakes also featured in the James Bond movie, *Quantum of Solace* which opens with a dramatic car chase in the tunnels along the eastern shore of Lake Garda, culminating in a spectacular crash.

Which lake?

There are six main holiday lakes, all quite different in character: Orta, Maggiore, Lugano, Como, Iseo and Garda (from west to east). German-orientated Lake Garda is the largest of the lakes and receives the most tourist visitors; its beaches, theme parks, sports and nightlife attract a younger crowd as well as families.

Lake Maggiore – famous for its jewel-like Borromean Islands and mountain-girt northern shores – is the second-largest lake, with its northern section lying in the Swiss canton of Ticino.

Stendhal was one of many literati who sang the praises of Lake Maggiore. In a letter to his younger sister in 1811 he wrote, 'When a man has a heart and a shirt, he should sell the shirt in order to see Lake Maggiore.'

Lovely little Lake Orta lies to the west and is noted for its spiritual air and excellent small hotels, while romantic Lake Como, north of Milan, offers dramatic scenery, quaint ports and *belle époque* villas. Captivating and tranquil Lake Iseo, between lakes Como and Garda, is the region's best-kept secret.

Villas and gardens

The **Baroque period** was a golden era for construction; ostentatious villas and gardens embodied the aspirations of ambitious owners. With its landscaped hillside gardens, Villa Carlotta on Lake Como exudes panache, while Lake Maggiore's Isola Bella, its grounds full of statuary, fountains and grottoes, is a triumph of lofty terraces. For the wealthy, there are palatial villas converted into luxury hotels, such as the Villa d'Este at Cernobbio and the Grand Hotel Villa Serbelloni at Bellagio. Wherever you go, the gardens are always sumptuous, with exotic flora that thrives in the benign spring-to-autumn climate.

Getting around

If you are planning to tour a number of lakes, renting a car is certainly the most convenient form of transport. However, driving along the lakeshores is not as leisurely as it may sound. Long stretches of the lakesides, including Como's eastern shore and much of Lake Maggiore's western one, are spoilt by heavy traffic along narrow and tortuous roads. Beware, too, of the dimly lit tunnels along the lakeshores. Cycling is hugely popular in the region; bikes are widely available for hire and can normally be taken on ferries. An increasing number of hiking routes have opened up, many with ravishing views of the lakes.

Autumn in Lake Varese

Castle at Arco

Lake trips by boat

Travelling on ferries is the most relaxing way of seeing the lakes. The first steamers on the lakes were launched in 1826, and boats have been ferrying passengers around ever since. In the early days most towns were without a landing stage, and rowing boats used to shuttle passengers and goods to and from the ferries. Today you can cruise around all the main lakes, stopping at almost every village. This is the best way to admire the fine mountain scenery and Riviera-like shores although rising prices are making it something of a luxury. The enclosed hydrofoils (*aliscafi*), which bypass the smaller ports, are the faster and more expensive means of travel, enabling you to cover the entire length of the larger lakes in two to three hours.

Getting high

Mountain cable-cars, whisking you from lakeside towns to mountain summits or ridges, provide another entertaining form of transport with truly spectacular views. You can take these from Como, and from Malcesine on Lake Garda. Bergamo has two funiculars, both well worth a trip: one connects the Città Bassa to the Città Alta, climbing 100m (330ft) from Viale Vittorio Emanuele II to the Piazza Mercato delle Scarpe – and taking you five hundred years back in time. The other links the Città Alta, beyond the Cittadella, to Colle San Vigilio. From here, you can climb to the top of Colle San Vigilio for the Castello, a ruined ancient stronghold, and a public park with fabulous views of Bergamo.

Milan

Few visitors to the region can resist a day's shopping trip to Milan. The city is synonymous with fashion and packs all the top designer stores in one very exclusive quarter near the centre of the city called the Quadrilatero d'Oro (Golden Quadrangle). But Milan has artistic and architectural treasures as well, among them Leonardo da Vinci's *The Last Supper*, the masterpieces in the Brera Art Gallery and one of the largest and most sumptuous Gothic churches in Europe.

Other historic cities

The southern stretches of the region are also home to artistically rich cities, such as Bergamo, Brescia, Mantua and Verona. With the exception of Verona, which is internationally renowned for its summer opera festival, which attracts massive numbers of visitors, these historic cities are comparatively free of crowds and commercialism, being bypassed by tourists making a beeline for Italy's more famous destinations. Easily accessed from the lakes, they make ideal destinations for day trips.

View of the castle in Malcesine, Lake Garda

Top tips for exploring the Italian Lakes

Trentino logo. When in Trentino, keep an eye out for the 'Osteria Tipica Trentina' signs, indicating restaurants that only serve seasonal local cuisine. These have to offer at least five Trentino cheeses, as well as local wines, grappa and mineral water.

Activities on Como. To take the effort out of arranging your own sports on Lake Como, contact The Orizzonti (www.orizzontilakecomo.com), which organises hiking, cycling and boat tours, horse-riding, caving and many more.

Ticket tip. Note that you can buy a combined entry ticket for both Isola Bella and Isola Madre from either Borromean island; it is cheaper than paying separately to visit each one.

Reserving for lunch. Restaurants in the region typically tend to be very busy, especially at lunchtime, so to avoid having to queue and, at worst, the disappointment of having to miss out altogether (especially if you have your heart set on eating at a particular restaurant), it's recommended to book a table in advance. To dine at one of the area's many Michelin-starred restaurants, be sure to book very well in advance. Note that Milan is a business city, so many of its restaurants close all day Saturday and at Sunday lunchtime. If in doubt, check before setting out.

Catching the ferry/ferry timetables. It may sound obvious, but when you consult ferry timetables, do make sure you pick the right ferry for the right day. Unless you are familiar with the timetables, the differentiation between weekday and Sunday/holiday travel is not immediately obvious, so do ask if you are unsure. To study timetables online in advance of travel see www.navigazionelaghi.it for Maggiore, Como and Garda, and www.navigazionelagoiseo.it for Iseo.

On your bike. Monte Isola is inundated with visitors in summer and at weekends but is a delight off-season. You can walk or cycle around the entire island on the lakeshore path (9km/5 miles), or hike up to the island's summit, which commands wonderful lake views. Bikes can be rented from Peschiera Maraglio or Carzano.

Restorative waters. The Italian medical profession insists that the lake climate is beneficial for 'the stressed and neurotic, the arthritic and the asthmatic, the elderly and young children'. As a result, the spas in the region are highly valued, especially those in Sirmione.

Dress appropriately. Remember to dress respectfully if you are visiting churches or other holy places. In some cases, this can mean no shorts, mini-skirts or vest tops.

Food and drink

The local cuisine, often enhanced by a mesmerising waterfront setting, is one of the great joys of travelling around the lakes. Regional dishes range from smoked hams and seasoned sausages to creamy risottos and fresh lake fish.

Lombard cuisine is highly varied, with ingredients sourced from lakes, mountains and flatlands. Rice, rather than pasta, is the mainstay of their diet; it is grown on the paddy fields of the Po Valley. Cream is very common, and butter tends to prevail over olive oil in local cooking. Lombardy also produces large quantities of corn, which is made into ubiquitous polenta. However, the lighter ingredients of the Mediterranean diet are also here: abundant fish, fresh fruit and vegetables – plus, of course, a glass or two of red wine.

Each region has its specialities. The Alpine influence can be seen in the array of cheeses, salami, polenta and mushroom dishes on offer in rural inns. The Austrian legacy around the north of Lake Garda has left the locals with a taste for veal, pork, beef, dumplings and gnocchi, while on the southern shore you will find roasts, stews, game and white truffles. Olive oil, oranges, lemons, peaches and pears represent a Mediterranean input. Milan may have moved towards more international tastes, such as sushi, but it still produces the famous *risotto alla milanese.*

Places to eat

The region is liberally endowed with restaurants, from simple tavernas to temples of gastronomy. These days there is little difference between a *ristorante, trattoria or osteria*. The region has many unpretentious *pizzerie*, often offering pasta, meat and fish as well. The best use wood-fired ovens *(forno a legna)*, but these are sometimes open only in the evening. You can often find places serving cheap slices of pizza *(al taglio)*, the favourite Italian takeaway.

Cafés and bars

Cafés are generally referred to in Italian as *bar*, which is actually the counter where coffees are served. Italians frequent bars at all times of day, from the breakfast *cappuccino* and *cornetto* to the late-night liqueur. Standing at the bar *(al banco)* is invariably cheaper than sitting at a table with waiter service. The pre-dinner *aperitivo*, from around 6-9pm, is a way of life in towns and

Mountain cheeses

resorts. The price of the drink may seem steep, but snacks, canapés and often a whole buffet are included in the price and can provide a cheap alternative to dinner in a restaurant. Cafés and bars offer a remarkable range of beverages: Prosecco or *spumante* (Italian sparkling wine, which you can have by the glass), spritz (Prosecco with Campari or Aperol), Negroni (Campari with vermouth and gin) and a long list of liqueurs and cocktails. An *enoteca* (wine bar) will offer a plate of sliced *prosciutto crudo*, salamis or cheeses to accompany its wide choice of wines.

Upmarket dining

You only have to see the stars studded across the region's maps in the Italy Michelin guide to realise how many gourmet restaurants there are here. The settings can be grandiose or minimalist, the food traditional or innovative, and many are sited in some of the region's most extravagant, romantically-sited hotels (see page 69).

Ordering your meal

Restaurant menus offer four courses: *antipasto*, the starter; *primo*, the first course, which is pasta, risotto or soup; *secondo*, the second course, such as fish or meat (accompanied perhaps by a *contorno*, a vegetable side dish); and finally, the *dolce* (dessert), or cheese and coffee. Don't feel pressurised into wading through all four courses; opting for just a couple – and not necessarily the *secondo* – is perfectly acceptable.

Food and drink prices

Throughout this book, we have used the following price guide for a two-course à la carte dinner for one with half a bottle of house wine.

€€€€ = €80 and above
€€€ = €50–80
€€ = €25–50
€ = under €25

What to eat

Regional risotto and ravioli

Thanks to the extensive rice fields on the Padua plain, risottos are abundant. Most famous of all, and served throughout the region, is *risotto alla milanese*, made with short-grain Arborio rice, slowly cooked with onions, beef marrow and stock, served with liberal amounts of butter and Parmesan cheese, and flavoured and coloured with saffron. Rice dishes can be enriched with fish, seafood, meat, wild *porcini* mushrooms, truffles or seasonal vegetables.

The other main *primo* is ravioli, stuffed perhaps with perch and parsley, black truffle, or ricotta or cottage cheese and basil. Look out for *cansonsèi* ravioli from the Bergamo and Brescia regions, or *tortelli di*

Pasta with anchovies and goats cheese

A sample menu

Vegetarians

There is an increasing number of restaurants offering at least one meat-and-fish-free dish, and with every year there are more establishments with vegan options. Where there are no main vegetarian dishes on offer, opt for a vegetable-based *antipasto* and *primo* (first course), but check first that stocks used for sauces are meat-free. Fresh, seasonal vegetables, often used to enrich pasta and risotto dishes, include *melanzane* (aubergines/eggplant), *carciofi* (artichokes), *zucchini* (courgettes), *radicchio* (red-leaved chicory), *funghi* (mushrooms) and *porcini* (wild boletus mushrooms).

zucca from Mantua: a sweet-and-sour pasta wrapped around puréed pumpkin and crushed amaretti, served with butter and Grana Padano.

Fish

Lake fish is plentiful and served in multiple ways. As an *antipasto*, it may come marinated, smoked, soused or puréed, as a *primo* it is added to pasta and risottos, and as a *secondo* it may be stuffed with vegetables and herbs, cooked in a sauce, or just grilled, fried or baked.

The most common species are *lavarello*, a white lake fish, perch *(persico)*, trout *(trota)*, pike *(luccio)* and char *(salmerino)*. Lake Iseo's speciality is *tinca ripiena*, baked tench stuffed with breadcrumbs, Parmesan and parsley and served with polenta. Around lakes Iseo and Como, menus may feature *missultini* (*or missultitt*); this is twaite shad, which has been stretched out on racks to dry in the sun, then grilled and served with olive oil and vinegar. On Lake Garda look out for the highly prized *carpione*, a type of carp, and *coregone in crosta*, a white fish flavoured with fennel and cooked in a salt crust.

Meat

Although fish is king around the lakes, most menus also offer a range of meat dishes. Along with simply cooked steak, pork, chicken or veal, you will find dishes of more humble origin: braised donkey, stewed tripe or, on the Padua plain, frogs' legs, eels and snails. The main Milanese specialities are *osso buco* (veal shank stew), *cotoletta alla milanese* (veal cutlet fried in breadcrumbs) and *cassoeula* (pork and cabbage casserole). Game features in the mountains, and in Trentino you will find Austrian-style sausages and sauerkraut, smoked hams and *speck*.

Cheese

The region excels in delicious cheeses, from tangy gorgonzola and pungent taleggio to creamy stracchino, robiola and mascarpone. Parmesan-like

A local pasticceria

Grana Padano, produced on the Padua plain, can be eaten sliced as an appetiser or part of a cheese platter, and is used in many pasta and risotto recipes. Market stalls have dozens of regional cheeses, marked *freschi* (fresh) or *stagionati* (mature). If in doubt, sample a cheese or two before buying.

What to drink

Wine and liqueurs

The DOC *(denominazione di origine controllata)* is an official mark of quality, but don't ignore the *vino da tavola* (house wine), which is often a good local wine. In more sophisticated establishments, you will be handed a hefty tome of wines, predominantly regional and national, but international too. Neighbouring Piedmont, Emilia-Romagna and the Veneto, all of which produce larger quantities of wine than Lombardy, will feature on most wine lists.

Although not one of Italy's great wine-producing regions, Lombardy has over a dozen wine-producing areas, and a quarter of the wine is DOC. The best of the red wine is produced on the steep slopes of the Valtellina in northern Lombardy: Grumello, Inferno, Sassella and Valgella. Franciacorta, south of Lake Iseo, is best known for sparkling spumante, made from Pinot and Chardonnay grapes. This is often drunk with fish in local restaurants as well as an *aperitivo*. From the shores of Lake Garda come the white Custoza and Lugana, the red Garda Valtenesi and the light, scented red and rosé Bardolinos.

A good meal is usually concluded with a *digestivo* (liqueur), such as a brandy, grappa or limoncello (made from lemons).

Coffee

If you want a small black coffee, ask for a *caffè*, or for a milky coffee, a *caffè latte* (ask for a 'latte' and you will probably get a glass of milk). This and *cappuccino* (or *cappuccio* as the locals call it) are only drunk at breakfast in Italy, although Italians are used to tourists asking for it at all times of day. A good halfway house is a *caffè macchiato*, an espresso with a dash of frothy milk in a small cup. If you want something with a real kick, order a *caffè doppio*, a double espresso; or after a meal, try a *caffè corretto*, with grappa, brandy or Sambuca added. For a good night's sleep forget the real thing and order a *caffè decaffeinato* or *decaff*.

Dessert

Dessert *(dolce)* is typically an almond or apple tart, or a cake, especially *tiramisù*, the alcoholic chocolate and coffee gateau. You may prefer to do as the Italians and buy an ice cream from the local *gelateria*, enjoying it while strolling down the street. After all, the Italians are said to make the best ice cream in the world.

Lake fish drying in the sun

Diners on the harbour in Bellagio

Shopping

The fact that most Italians now use the expression *'fare lo shopping'* may suggest a globalisation of the shopping scene. But the advent of shopping malls has barely dented the popularity of boutiques, gourmet food shops and markets.

Style and elegance are reflected in the chic stores of Milan, one of the world's fashion powerhouses, and, to a lesser extent, in smaller cities such as Como ('City of Silk') and Bergamo. The lakeside towns and villages offer less choice and higher prices, but an altogether more relaxed shopping experience.

Food and drink

Small food shops throughout the lakes region display a wide variety of tempting delicacies, from home-cured hams and handmade pastas to herbs and honey to local wines and liqueurs. Milan's temple of deli gastronomy is the legendary Peck (Via Spadari 9; www.peck.it), a stunning showcase of cheeses, hams, truffles and foie gras. The shores of Lake Garda offer locally grown and pressed aromatic olive oil, Bardolino wines and Limoncello liqueur made from local lemons, while the winegrowing Franciacorta region produces the best fizz in Italy.

Markets

Weekly markets are colourful open-air affairs, with stalls selling flowers, food, fashions, household goods and more. Every Wednesday, Luino on Lake Maggiore hosts what it claims to be the biggest weekly market in Europe, with bargain-hunters descending from Switzerland, Austria and Germany as well as Italy. Monthly antique markets are a source of local handicrafts, although real bargains are rare. Nevertheless, bargaining, even if only in broken Italian, is always worth a try.

Fashion in Milan

Since the 1980s Milan has been a world centre for fashion design, drawing huge numbers of visitors – many celebrities among them – to its Fashion Weeks and the flagship stores of Armani, Prada and other top designers. At the opening of Fashion Weeks (AW Feb/Mar, SS Sept/Oct) the international paparazzi descend on the city, while the hip hotels and stylish restaurants are packed with celebrities and supermodels.

The flagship outlets of the big designer names are conveniently concentrated in a small, attractive

Shopping street in Bellagio

area, known as the Quadrilatero d'Oro (Golden Quadrangle). Stores range from chic little boutiques to modern emporia such as Armani, complete with restaurant, bookstore, flower shop and furnishings, as well as fashions.

Prices are not for the faint-hearted, but if your credit card can't stretch to cutting-edge collections, there are plenty of more affordable fashions in the city centre, as well as the arty boutiques of the Brera and Ticinese quarters.

Como silk

Como, centre of Italy's silk industry, has produced silk and other textiles since the 15th century. Silkworms are no long longer bred here, but Chinese fibres are imported to be woven, dyed, designed and printed. Top designers still depend on Como for their silk but the industry has been in steady decline over the decades, with competition from China, and increasingly high prices of silk as Chinese farmers turn to more lucrative crops. Como shops no longer dazzle with Como silk but you can still find ties and scarves – and a museum (see page 12) that documents the story of this fascinating industry.

Factory outlets

The lakes region has a number of *'outlets'* (discount factory stores), selling seductive clothes, cult-design icons, crafts, leatherware and gourmet gifts. One of the few surviving silk outlets around Como is Frey Emporio della Seta in Fino Mornasco (Via Risorgimento 49; www.frey.it), southwest of Como which sells hand-painted silk scarves, shirts and ties of top designers with good discounts. At the Foxtown Outlet (www.foxtown.com) in the Swiss village of Mendrisio 15km (6 miles) northeast of Como you can snap up brands such as Gucci, Versace, Dolce & Gabbana and Prada. Silk manufacturer Mantero – supplier to Yves Saint Laurent, Calvin Klein and other big names – has a small shop here. The functional but well-designed Franciacorta Outlet Village (Rodengo Saiano, 7km/4.5 miles west of Brescia; (www.franciacortavillage.it) has over 160 stores. Armani fans should head for its outlet at Vertemate, south of Como, which has some great bargains in its warehouse.

Bergamo

In the heart of the region, Bergamo is a delightful city for shopping as well as sightseeing. The upper town has some lovely food shops and clothes boutiques, while Il Sentierone and Via XX Settembre in the lower town have fashions, silk, leather goods and jewellery. A shuttle bus service links the upper and lower towns with the airport just 5km (3 miles) away, which is opposite the huge Orio shopping centre (www.oriocenter.it).

Shoe shop in Salò

Silk ties from Como

Entertainment

The lakeside towns are peaceful places by night, favouring leisurely dinners, lakeside strolls and a liqueur at a local bar. But entertainment is never far away with the clubs of Brescia and Bergamo to the opera or Milan's hip bars.

The Lombardy region has a strong musical tradition. Violinmaker Stradivarius and composer Monteverdi both came from Cremona, Donizetti was born and died in Bergamo, and Verdi composed *La Traviata* while staying on Lake Como. Today opera, concerts and music festivals take place in cities across the region and in castles, villas and other historic locations around the lakes.

Festivals and events

The lakes and Lombard cities stage some of the finest events on the Italian cultural calendar. Events take place all year round and include classical music festivals, boat processions, food and wine fairs, fireworks over the lake and jazz extravaganzas.

The most prestigious festival of the lakes is Stresa's **Settimane Musicali** (www.stresafestival.eu), running from mid-July through September with a programme of classical, jazz concerts with internationally renowned musicians, performed in churches, historical venues and even some wonderful outdoor spaces. Founded in 1961, it has expanded from Stresa to towns and villages all around Lake Maggiore. Events feature the festival's own resident orchestra, as well as renowned international musicians.

Gardone Riviera on Lake Garda presents drama, opera and concerts in the evocative open-air amphitheatre of the Vittoriale degli Italiani in July and August (www.anfiteatrodelvittoriale.it) while Riva del Garda hosts a choral festival in March.

The tiny wine-producing region of Franciacorta south of Lake Iseo stages a sparkling wine and food festival in September, along with wine- and food-tasting events in the vineyards at weekends (www.stradadelfranciacorta.it). The Grape and Wine Festival at Bardolino (famed for its red wine) on Lake Garda is another cork-popping event held in the autumn. This is the time to buy quantities of wine very cheaply.

Festival of San Giovanni

One of the most ancient and magical lake festivals is that of San

Classic-car rally in the lakes

Giovanni (St John), celebrated at Isola Comacina, Lake Como, on the weekend closest to St John the Baptist's Day (24 June). Mass is held in the church ruins, and thousands of bobbing boats are illuminated by candles and fireworks, creating spectacular views. For some of the best views, you can join a night cruise with onboard dinner and dancing. For those eager to immerse themselves fully in this timeless festival, seeking guidance from your accommodation is beneficial. Hotel staff, well-versed in the nuances of the event, can provide invaluable insights.

Opera in Verona

If you are staying on the south or east side of Lake Garda, try to take in an opera extravaganza in nearby Verona's great Roman amphitheatre. The experience is an unforgettable one, and you don't have to be an opera buff to enjoy it. The lavish, open-air performances take place from mid-June to the beginning of September, and the operas alternate, so that in one month you have a choice of three or four different performances. Book well in advance on www.arena.it.

Nightlife

Milan apart, the region is not really renowned for discos and nightclubs. Garda is the liveliest of the lakes, particularly in the town of Desenzano del Garda, where bars, live music and nightclubs attract a younger crowd.

Como, although not exactly a hot spot, has some sociable late-opening bars along the Lungo Lario Trieste waterfront.

Bergamo offers upmarket wining and dining, classical concerts and plenty of bars, but for nightclubs, you need to head out of town.

Milan

Milan offers some of the most vibrant nightlife in Italy, with a huge range of classical concerts, theatre, live jazz and rock, pop concerts and scores of stylish *aperitivo* bars and nightclubs. It is also home to La Scala (www.teatroallascala.org), one of the world's most prestigious opera houses (see page 99). If you want to attend a performance, it's advisable (and often essential) to book well in advance. The coolest places to be and be seen move with the speed of light – the best option is to target the areas which have the most interesting scenes and take your pick. As well as iconically fashionable Brera and the buzzing Navigli canal area, have a look around the up-and-coming arty-hipster quarter, Isola the recently redesigned area around Porta Garibaldi station.

Salò by night

La Scala

Activities

Lake Garda is a sporting paradise, boasting windsurfing, sailing, hiking and cycling, while at Ascona on Lake Maggiore, you can ski in the morning and then play a leisurely round of golf in the afternoon.

Watersports

Lake Garda has countless sailing regattas, including world championships. Riva del Garda and Torbole have numerous watersports schools with gear to rent and tuition for all levels. On Lake Maggiore, Laveno, Luino, Ascona and Locarno are bases for sailing and windsurfing. On Lake Como the town of Como offers sailing, water-skiing, diving and canoeing, while further up the lake at Menaggio and Bellagio you can water-ski and hire motorboats, canoes or kayaks. Lakeside lidos and pebbly 'beaches' are popular in high season. Bellagio's revamped lido comes with a beach bathing area, sunbeds, cocktail bar and nightlife.

Hiking and climbing

Ridges above the lakes, woodland trails and the Alpine mountains provide wonderful scenery and cater for all levels of hiking fitness. At Torbole and Riva del Garda freeclimbers hang above the lake, and Arco, further north, has hosted international climbing and paraclimbing championships.

On Lake Garda the Monte Baldo ridge has clear trails and fine views, as does Monte Mottarone above Lake Maggiore. Both have cable-car access (from Stresa and Malcesine, respectively).

For hikes in the Alps, the best months are May to October. The Club Alpino Italiano or CAI (Italian Alpine Club; www.cai.it) organises guided tours, provides maps and runs shelters for hikers. Many of the routes are not as well marked or developed as in other European countries, and for serious hiking you may want to hire one of their local guides.

Cycling and mountain biking

Lombardy alone has nearly 700 cycling clubs and 1,200 annual races. Every May, 20,000 mountain bikers descend on Riva del Garda for the Bike Festival, a celebration of all things MTB (and eMTB) with exhibitions, shows, competitions, excursions, and stunts. For a thrilling ride down a mountain without the uphill struggle, take a bike on the cable-car up to Monte Baldo.

The steep hill of the Madonna del Ghisallo (12km/7.5 miles south of Bellagio) serves as a challenging last lap of a number of national and local cycling races. Thousands of cyclists and visitors come here annually – and not

Kite surfer on Lake Garda in Campione

just for the panoramic views of Lake Como. At the top of the hill is a church dedicated to the Madonna del Ghisallo, who in 1949 was declared the patroness of cyclists by official papal edict. The church then became a cycling museum, displaying bikes and equipment of cycling champions, historic models, trophies and other memorabilia. The state-of-the-art three-storey Museo del Ciclismo (Cycling Museum, www.museodelghisallo.it; charge) beside the church houses some of the exhibits.

Golf

Lakes Maggiore, Como and Garda have golf courses, many with wonderful views. Some of the finest are around Franciacorta and Lake Garda: the Franciacorta Golf Club (www.franciacortagolfclub.it) is to the south of Lake Iseo, while Bogliaco Golf Resort (www.golfbogliaco.com) and Garda Golf (www.gardagolf.it) are both to the west of Lake Garda between Salò and Desenzano del Garda. The oldest club is the Menaggio and Cadennabia Golf Club (www.menaggio.it) at Lake Como, which was set up by four Englishmen in the late 19th century. Another prestigious location is the Villa d'Este Golf Club (www.villadeste.com).

Extreme sports

Paragliding is popular on Monte Baldo, near Malcesine (www.paraglidingclubmalcesine.it) Lake Garda's winds are ideal for kitesurfing. The Stickl Sportcamp (www.stickl.com) organises courses in surfing sailing kitesurfing and foiling for all levels, communicating with kitesurfers through radio receivers fitted into the helmets.

Rock-climbing

The northern end of Lake Garda, where walls rise to 1,200m (3,900ft), is a haven for rock climbers . Arco, just north of Torbole, has Europe's largest open-air wall and hosts the Rock Master free-climbing world championships in September. This unique destination not only attracts seasoned climbers but also offers a vibrant atmosphere for enthusiasts and spectators alike during the thrilling international climbing competition, creating a true celebration of the sport amidst the dramatic setting.

Skiing

Snow permitting, you can ski and snowboard at Monte Baldo on Lake Garda, Monte Mottarone, Passo Forcora and Cardada on Lake Maggiore, and Piani di Bobbio above Lecco on Lake Como. These stunning alpine locations offer a diverse range of slopes and breath-taking panoramas, making them ideal destinations for winter sports enthusiasts seeking both adventure and scenic beauty. Whether you're a seasoned skier or a snowboarding aficionado, these picturesque spots provide an exhilarating experience against the backdrop of Italy's remarkable lakeside landscapes.

Cycling is a true passion here

Chronology

The lakes' proximity to the great trade routes between the Mediterranean and Central Europe ensured prosperity and enticed foreign invasion. Each new arrival made its mark, contributing a rich history and culture to this fine region.

Early history

8,000BC Emergence of the Valle Camonica civilisation, with the first rocks carved by Camuni tribes.
202–191BC Romans start to establish colonies in Milan, Como, Brescia, Verona and other settlements.
222BC Romans conquer Milan.
AD313 Emperor Constantine grants freedom of worship to Christians in the Edict of Milan.
4th century Milan becomes the de facto capital of the western Roman Empire.
568 The Lombards establish their capital at Pavia.

The Middle Ages

774 Charlemagne takes the Lombard crown.
1024 Emergence of the comuni, or independent city-states.
1118–27 Como defeated by Milan in the Ten Years War.
1152 German prince Frederick Barbarossa is named as the Holy Roman Emperor.
1260–1387 Lake Garda and Verona ruled by Scaligeri (della Scala) dynasty.
1277–1447 Duchy of Milan ruled by the Visconti dynasty.
1347–8 Black Death devastates the population of northern Italy.
1405 Venetians conquer Verona, Padua and Bergamo.
1450–99 Duchy of Milan ruled by the Sforza dynasty.

Foreign intervention

1530 Charles V is crowned as the Holy Roman Emperor, and Lombardy comes under his rule.
1714 Spain cedes Lombardy to the Austrian (Habsburg) empire.
1796 Napoleon invades northern Italy.
1814–70 The Risorgimento – a movement for the liberation and political unification of Italy.
1848 Milanese rebel against the Austrians, who re-enter the city.
1859 France defeats Austria at the battles of Magenta and Solferino.
1871 Italian unification.

20th century

1915 Italy joins the World War I Allies.
1922 Mussolini becomes prime minister, and within three years has

Battle of Solferino in 1859

Giorgia Meloni

established a dictatorship and declared himself Il Duce.

1940 Italy enters World War II as an ally of Nazi Germany.

1943–5 Italy surrenders to the Allies; Mussolini is installed in the Republic of Salò.

1945 Mussolini and his mistress, Claretta Petacci, are captured by partisans and executed.

1958 Italy joins the EEC, forerunner of the European Union (EU).

1978 Aldo Moro, ex-prime minister and leader of the Christian Democrats, kidnapped and murdered by the left-wing Red Brigade.

1992 Tangentopoli ('Bribesville') corruption scandals rock the north and lead to an overhaul of public life.

21st century

2001 Silvio Berlusconi is elected prime minister.

2002 The euro replaces the lira as the official Italian currency.

2008 Berlusconi starts his fourth term as Prime Minister.

2011 Mario Monti brought in as PM to rescue Italy from the debt crisis.

2013 Pope Benedict XVI resigns and is succeeded by Pope Francis I.

2013 The anti-establishment Five Star Movement, co-founded by ex-comedian Beppe Grillo, stuns the mainstream parties by taking a quarter of the votes in the general election.

2016 A series of severe earthquakes occur in Central Italy, causing extensive damage, injuries and deaths.

2017 Italy fails to qualify for the 2018 FIFA World Cup, the first time since 1958.

2022 Right-winger Giorgia Meloni is elected Prime Minister on an anti-immigration ticket. Migrant figures – and deaths at sea – continue to rise.

2023 Devastating floods in Emilia Romagna; wildfires and record-breaking temperatures in southern Italy; freak storms in Lombardy.

Lake Como in 1830

BEST ITINERARIES

Tour 1: The Borromean Islands **30**
Tour 2: Stresa and Angera Castle **34**
Tour 3: Monte Mottarone and Santa Caterina .. **38**
Tour 4: Villa Taranto and Lake Mergozzo **40**
Tour 5: Lake Maggiore Express **44**
Tour 6: Lake Orta **48**
Tour 7: Varese and Lake Lugano **52**
Tour 8: Villa Carlotta and Bellagio **56**
Walk 9: Como Town and Brunate Cable-car **60**
Tour 10: Ramo di Como and Villa del Balbianello **64**
Walk 11: Bergamo **70**
Tour 12: Lake Iseo **74**
Tour 13: The Franciacorta Wine Trail **79**
Walk 14: Sirmione **82**
Tour 15: Lake Garda Cruise **86**
Tour 16: Gardone Riviera **90**
Tour 17: A Taste of Trentino **94**
Walk 18: Milan **98**

TOUR 1
The Borromean Islands

An island-hopping day trip from the resort of Stresa to Isola Bella, Isola dei Pescatori and Isola Madre within Lake Maggiore. Explore the villas and grounds of these three exotic outcrops, lunching in a fish restaurant on Isola dei Pescatori.

DISTANCE: 13km (8 miles) return trip by ferry
TIME: A full day
START/END: Stresa
POINTS TO NOTE: Regular ferries operate from Stresa to the islands. Pick up a timetable from the ferry station or check times on www.navigazionelaghi.it. If you do not want the restrictions of a timetable – the ferry service stops early evening – consider taking one of the not-too-extortionate private boats by the ferry station. The islands are packed throughout the season; make an early start if you want to see all three islands in a day and avoid the worst of the crowds.

Located off the shore of Stresa (see page 34), the Borromean Islands lie at the centre of Lake Maggiore, which, despite its name, is the second-largest Italian lake after Garda. The long, narrow ribbon of water stretches 65km (40 miles) and is bordered by Lombardy to the east, Piedmont to the west and the Swiss canton of Ticino to the north. The scenery varies from the wild northern mountains, where the Swiss pre-Alps descend towards the lake, to the gentler Mediterranean-like shores of the south.

Isola Bella

At the ferry station on Piazza Marconi, beside the tourist office, you can buy a ticket that includes entrances to the island sights. Alight at the first stop – Isola Bella.

Whereas Isola dei Pescatori was styled as a rural retreat and Isola Madre as an enchanted garden, **Isola Bella ❶** (www.borromeoturismo.it; charge) was always intended to be a showy pleasure palace. In recent times Isola Bella has served as the Borromean princes' summer residence; the family stays in the island palace. To protect the family's privacy and its impressive art collection, two-thirds of the palace is closed to the public, but it is still worth seeing, not least for the beguiling Baroque gardens and the palatial treasures on show.

Lake Maggiore

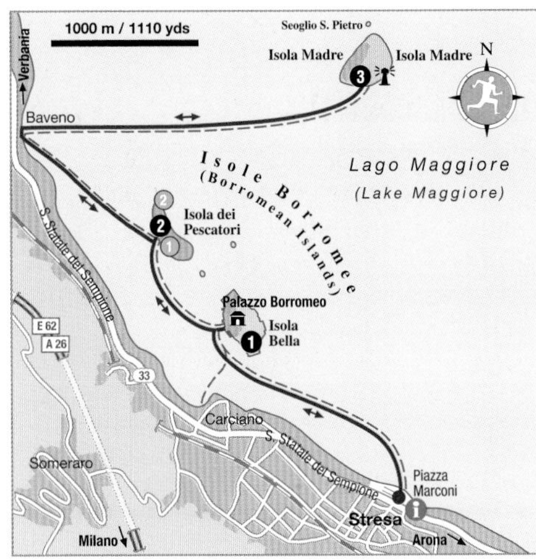

original plans, family descendants continued to embellish the island until the 1950s when Vitiliano IX, the last member of the family to attempt major modifications, died before building his cherished harbour.

From a rock to a monument

Although Isola Bella began as little more than a rocky islet with a view, over the course of centuries it became a delightful folly. In the 1620s Count Carlo III Borromeo was inspired to create a full-blown monument to his wife Isabella. To realise his vision the rocks were transformed into an island with ten terraces designed to resemble the prow of a ship in full sail. Boatloads of soil were transported to this barren island, as well as Baroque statuary and the building materials needed for the creation of a palatial villa. The works continued under his son, Vitiliano VI, and were virtually complete by the time of his death in 1670. Even so, inspired by the

Borromean Palace

The island creates a dramatic impact as you approach. Disembarking from the ferry, follow the flow to the turreted **Palazzo Borromeo**. The stern façade belies a lavish interior, full of gilt and stuccowork, marble statues and Murano chandeliers. The palace's high-ceilinged rooms contain a fine collection of 16th- to 18th-century northern Italian art, though it is encrusted in a Baroque clutter of stuccowork and heraldic crests, only partially redeemed by bold flourishes such as a cantilevered spiral staircase. Lavishly overstuffed public rooms connect a gilded throne room, an empire-style ballroom and a Flemish long gallery housing tapestries emblazoned with the unicorns that adorn the dynasty's distinctive crest.

The palace has witnessed numerous momentous historical events, and has played host to emperors and statesmen.

View of the Borromean Islands

In 1797 Napoleon slept in one of the bedrooms – a ponderous Neoclassical chamber decorated in what was the politically correct Directoire style. The ornate music room was the setting for the Stresa peace conference of 1935: it was here that Italy, Britain and France failed to agree on a strategic response to Hitler's programme of rapid rearmament, a missed opportunity that hastened the momentum towards war.

Grottoes and garden

Designed as a cool summer retreat, the area beneath the palace conceals bizarre artificial **grottoes**, with tufa-stone walls studded with shells, pebbles and fossils. The maritime mood is sustained in the statue of a coolly reclining nude and caverns dotted with marine imagery. This grotesque creation reflects the contemporary taste for *Wunderkammer* – chambers of marvels designed to enchant visitors with their eclectic displays. In the case of Isola Bella, however, the greatest marvel lies outside.

The Baroque **gardens** envelop the palace in sweeping arcs, with dramatic architectural perspectives accentuated by grandiose urns, obelisks, fountains and statues. Although the terraced gardens abound in arbours, water features and statuary, the sum is greater than its parts. Serried ranks of orange and lemon trees meet flower beds before fading into a studied confusion of camellias and magnolias, laurels, cypresses, jasmine and pomegranate.

The ship-shaped **terraces**, crowned by a four-tiered folly studded with shells and topped by cherubs and classical gods, culminate in a huge statue of a heraldic unicorn. It is all rather pompous, but you can't fail to admire the variety of exotic flora, and the sublime views across to Monte Mottarone. The pièce de résistance is a shell-shaped **amphitheatre** that serves as a delightful setting for summer concerts.

After your visit return to the ferry landing stage (the rest of the island is awash with trinket stands and poor-quality tourist restaurants).

Isola dei Pescatori

A five-minute ferry ride from Isola Bella brings you to **Isola dei Pescatori** ❷, or as you hear the ferrymen announce it, 'Isola Superiore dei Pescatori'. The full name derives from the Latin *superior*, indicating that it is further north than Isola Bella (Isola Inferiore).

The island is a pretty fishing village less dedicated to fishing than to the preservation of its film-set picturesque appearance. It is a place for pottering down tiny alleys and peering at the lake, or even paddling off the pebble beach facing Isola Bella. The maze of passageways conjures up the mood of a remote Greek island. Henry James praised this pocket of Italy for making one feel 'out of the rush and crush of the modern world'.

Statue on Isola Bella

Lunch break

Of the three islands the Isola dei Pescatori is the best bet for lunch, with two inviting waterside restaurants serving fresh fish: the **Hotel Ristorante Verbano**, see ①, adjoining the pebble beach, or the **Hotel Ristorante Belvedere**, see ②, five minutes' walk north.

After lunch take the next ferry to Isola Madre, which stops at the resort of Baveno en route.

Isola Madre

Enjoy the cooling breezes on the ferry to **Isola Madre** ❸ (www.borromeoturismo.it; charge). Here on the largest of the islands, and what was once the wildest, you will find gently landscaped gardens. The island is home to Europe's largest Kashmiri cypress and some of the first camellias planted in Italy. Best seen in spring, the camellias are part of a patchwork formed by shady paths, ancient cedars, mimosa, magnolias and giant rhododendrons, and populated by white peacocks, Chinese pheasants and parrots. The best time to visit is April for camellias or May for azaleas and rhododendrons. In 2006 a freak storm uprooted the island's great Kashmiri Cypress tree. A huge rescue effort, involving cranes brought over by helicopter and ropes to secure it, seems to have paid off, as new growth is showing.

Food and Drink

① Hotel Ristorante Verbano
Via Ugo Ara 2, Isola dei Pescatori; www.hotelverbano.it
Gourmet restaurant with several themed tasting menus (including a vegetarian option) set on a lakeside terrace overlooking Isola Bella that is especially fine in the evenings. Fish-based cuisine. €€€€

② Hotel Ristorante Belvedere
Via di Mezzo, Isola dei Pescatori; www.belvedere-isolapescatori.it
An idyllic waterside setting with meals served in the garden, on the veranda or in the lakeview dining room. The emphasis is on lake fish. Free evening boat service from/to Stresa. €€

The 16th-century **villa** – an apparently austere Mannerist affair created as a home rather than a palace – is a bit stifling and gloomy. The Borromean family indulged their love of theatre here – check out the curious collection of puppet theatres, puppets and dolls.

In the evening you could also dine on Isola dei Pescatori – it is at its most romantic when the crowds have gone. Otherwise, return to Stresa, bearing in mind the last ferry departs at around 6.30pm.

The Baroque gardens of Palazzo Borromeo

TOUR 2
Stresa and Angera Castle

This tour combines a stroll in Stresa, 'Queen of the Lake', with a cruise of the southern section of Lake Maggiore, alighting at Angera for a leisurely fish lunch and the finest fortress on the lake.

DISTANCE: Walk in Stresa: 3km (2 miles); cruise to Angera and back: 32km (20 miles)
TIME: A leisurely full day
START/END: Stresa
POINTS TO NOTE: Ferry timetables – and any warnings about weather, strikes or cancellations – are on www.nagigazionelaghi.com. Services between Stresa and Angera are spasmodic – so plan in advance – and the last boat back from Angera to Stresa leaves mid-afternoon.

Stresa

The main resort on the Piedmontese shore, **Stresa** ❶ was a *belle époque* wintering ground, the popularity of which was enhanced by the opening of the Simplon Pass in 1906. This allowed a railway from the other side of the Alps, giving Stresa instant access.

A dowager resort that is perhaps past its prime, Stresa is considered to be the noble part of Lake Maggiore. It found favour with both Queen Victoria and Winston Churchill and remains popular with superannuated politicians and former world leaders. It may have lost the cachet it once enjoyed as one of the most fashionable A-list resorts in Europe, but as a base on the lake, the resort still can't be beaten for views, excursions and easy access to the Borromean Islands.

Lakeside promenade

From Stresa's bustling waterfront at Piazza Marconi take the **lakeside promenade** northwest towards the sandy Lido. The main road divides the garden-lined promenade from the succession of imposing hotels and elegant villas. Replete with beguiling vistas over the Borromean Islands, the lakeside rose gardens have a sedate air that complements the resort's genteel reputation.

The 15-minute stroll towards Baveno passes Stresa's grandest hotels, the sole relic of its *fin de siècle* heyday. The 18th-century **Villa Ducale**, where the philosopher

Stunning view of the Rocca di Angera, Lake Maggiore

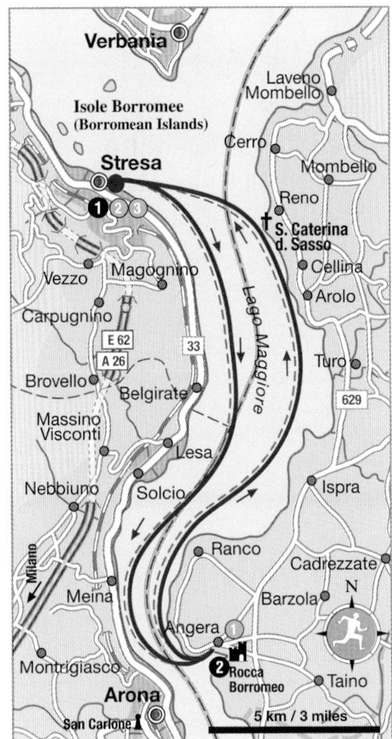

Antonio Rosmini died in 1855 (and which is now the Rosmini Study Centre) gives way to the Art Nouveau Regina Palace hotel and its renowned restaurant, followed by the **Grand Hôtel des Iles Borromées**, where several literary luminaries have stayed over the years (see page 105). Among them was Ernest Hemingway, who recuperated here after being wounded in battle and then used the resort as a backdrop in *A Farewell to Arms* (1929). At the end of the promenade, you come to the Lido (see page 38).

Cruise to Angera

During the cruise you will pass Stresa's Neoclassical **Villa Pallavicino**, with landscaped grounds and an appealing zoo, and the delightful village of **Belgirate**. Further south, towards Arona, are clusters of exclusive villas belonging to various celebrities, especially around **Meina**.

Angera and Rocca Borromeo

In **Angera,** the medieval hulk of the **Rocca Borromeo** ❷ (Via alla Rocca; www.isoleborromee.it; charge), dominating the town, soon looms into view. In the 11th century, the twin fortresses of Arona and Angera were built to safeguard the strategic southern part of the lake. Arona's fortress was destroyed by Napoleon. Angera's, the best-preserved castle on the lake, became the property of the Milanese Visconti in the late 13th century, but in 1450 it passed to the Borromean dynasty, who converted it into a residence and have owned it ever since. The Visconti covered the walls with frescoes celebrating the glory and longevity of their dynasty. The Gothic **Sala di Giustizia** (Hall of Justice), a vaulted chamber, is adorned with signs of the zodiac

Angling at dusk

San Carlone

The Rocca Borromeo, like the Borromean Islands off Stresa, belongs to the Borromeo dynasty. A famous member of the family was San Carlo (St Charles), who was born in 1538 in the (now-ruined) castle of Arona and devoted his life to the reform and welfare of the Church. A meteoric rise to power saw him become a cardinal at the age of 22 and archbishop of Milan at 26. Carlo founded seminaries and religious colleges and worked ceaselessly during the plague of 1576–8, accommodating the sick, burying the dead and risking his own health in doing so. He was canonised posthumously by Pope Paul V in 1610. A huge statue of the saint, familiarly known as San Carlone (big St Charles), stands above Arona. You can climb right up inside the statue and look through his eyes – though it is stifling to do so on a hot summer's day. The grounds of the Rocca are usually open to the public on Fridays and Saturdays.

and scenes of military victories. For fine views over the lake, climb the steps up the **Torre Principale**, then enjoy the enchanting **Medieval Gardens**, created in 2008, with a stream running through woods, a fabulous rose garden and hundreds of herbs and other plants grown for their essential oils.

Doll Museum

A dozen rooms of the castle are devoted to the **Museo della Bambola** (www.museobambola-santagiuletta.it; charge), one of the largest collections of dolls in Europe. Dating from the 18th to the 20th century, the dolls are remarkably detailed and varied; they are made of everything from wood and wax to papier mâché, fabric and plastic. The collection also features dolls' furniture, toys, board games and children's clothes from the 18th century, plus fully functioning late 19th- and early 20th-century French and German automatons (1870–1920).

Lunch with a view

For lunch the best option is the lakeside **Hotel Lido**, see 1.

This is the narrowest section of Lake Maggiore, and, mists permitting, there should be good views across to **Arona** on the Piedmontese shore. Towering over the town is the **San Carlone** – a colossal statue of the locally born, beatified reformer San Carlo Borromeo (1538–84) – which, when built, was the world's tallest statue after New York's Statue of Liberty.

Grand Hotel Bristol in Stresa, Lake Maggiore

Food and Drink

① Hotel Lido
Viale Libertà 11, Angera;
www.hotellido.it
A good fish restaurant within a lakeshore hotel. Try the artichoke and anchovy salad, spaghetti with Romanesco and calamari or tagliolini with lemon and burrata. Good wine list, but they also recommend wines by the glass to suit each dish. €€

② La Botte
Via Mazzini 6/8, Stresa;
www.trattorialabottlestresa.it
'The Barrel' is a tiny wood-panelled, ambient, chef-owned restaurant in a narrow street located just a minute's walk from the main piazza. Dishes include seasonal specialities (the menu changes every two months), and good pasta. Try the ravioli with trout and samphire or the mixed fried lake fish. Reservations are recommended due to its popularity. €

③ Bistrot 76
Via Mazzini 25, Stresa;
www.ristorantepiemontese.com
A long-established Stresa restaurant with a delightful setting and friendly atmosphere. Meals are taken in the cosy dark-wood interior or the vine-covered terrace. Excellent food – look out for black truffle dishes – and choice wines. €€

Back to Stresa

Stresa is short of specific sights, but it does possess a certain faded charm, from a tiny harbour full of fishing boats to bustling **Piazza Cadorna**, the main inland square. It's a popular tourist destination known for its stunning natural scenery and laid-back atmosphere. Stresa is a particularly lovely place to be in the evening. Go for a wander *(passeggiata)* then sit down under the plane trees and sip a drink in **Caffè Nazionale** or get an ice cream at the nearby **Angolo del Gelato** to accompany your stroll.

This is prime shopping time, so you could saunter down Via Bolognaro to see the old-fashioned shops, or continue to Via Garibaldi, parallel with the lakeshore, which has a reliable pastry shop-Pasticceria Caffetteria Bravi at No. 6. If planning a picnic for the following day, call in at Stresa's main supermarket, Carrefour, located at Via Roma 11, just off Piazza Cadorna.

For dinner head to **La Botte**, see ②, or **Bistrot 76**, see ③, both on Via Mazzini, the street linking Piazza Cadorna and Piazza Matteotti.

The ceiling at the Rocca Borromeo

Colossus of San Carlo Borromeo, a massive bronze statue

TOUR 3
Monte Mottarone and Santa Caterina

Climb the Monte Mottarone peak, a natural balcony that overlooks the Alps and lakes; then take a ferry to Santa Caterina del Sasso, an enchanting medieval hermitage that clings to a cliff by Lake Maggiore.

DISTANCE: Walking: 1.5km (1 mile); ferry return trip 9km (5.5 miles)
TIME: A full day
START/END: Stresa
POINTS TO NOTE: Between lakes Maggiore and Orta, the Mottarone peak commands a wonderful panorama of the lakes and Alps. A road leads up there from Gignese but be warned: you will have to pay several euros to get there, as the last section is a toll road. You can also access the peak on foot, and then walk down to Orta. Choose a clear day for Monte Mottarone and take something warm to wear. Check out afternoon ferry times to and from Santa Caterina (there is at least one an hour) and note the time of the last boat. There are no midday boats from Stresa, and for a leisurely visit you need to get the earliest afternoon ferry and return on the penultimate or last boat. There is no café at Santa Caterina, so lunch on Monte Mottarone or in Stresa. An alternative would be to drive on from Monte Mottarone to Lake Orta (see page 48).

Between lakes Maggiore and Orta, Monte Mottarone (1,491m/4,891ft) commands a magnificent panorama of misty lakes, snow-crested peaks and the Po Valley. On one of the rare clear days the view stretches to seven lakes. However, following a fatal accident in 2021, the cable-car remains closed, and with investigations continuing as we write in 2023, it may remain so for some years.

Access by car

Mottarone can also be reached by car (take the road to Gignese from central Stresa). The last section of the road is owned by the Borromeo family, and you will have to pay a toll.

You can also get to Santa Caterina by car in about an hour. From Stresa drive to Intra (18km/11 miles), then take the Intra–Laveno car ferry (20 mins), and drive from Laveno to Santa Caterina (5km/3 miles). A short walk from the car park are the 268 steep steps down to the church.

Monte Mottarone

On the drive up Monte Mottarone, it is worth making a diversion

Santa Caterina del Sasso monastery

(signposted from Gignese) to see the rock gardens of the **Giardino Botanico Alpinia** (Alpine Botanical Garden; www.giardinobotanicoalpinia.altervista.org; charge), with over 1,000 species of Alpine and medicinal plants. The latest family attraction is the panoramic **Alpyland** ❶ coaster (www.alpyland.com; charge), where you can ride bobsleighs at speeds of up to 40kph (25mph) come snow or sunshine. Just down the road is **Casa della Neve**, see ①, where you can admire the views and grab a bite to eat.

Santa Caterina del Sasso

Return to Stresa and go to Piazza Marconi, where ferries for Santa Caterina leave from the main landing stage. It is only a 15-minute trip, then from the landing stage you have to climb up eighty steps.

The Carmelite convent of **Santa Caterina del Sasso** ❷ (the Hermitage; www.santacaterinadelsasso.com; charge), seemingly suspended over a rocky precipice and overhung by crags, is at its most romantic when viewed from the lake. Set on the only stretch of Lake Maggiore that has no banks, the Hermitage, which is renowned for its Gothic frescoes, guards the deepest parts of the lake. According to legend, it was founded by Alberto Besozzi, a shipwrecked 12th-century moneylender who vowed to become a hermit if he survived.

In 1195 Besozzi's piety was said to have been instrumental in averting a plague, and he was rewarded with the building of a hermitage to the 3rd-century St Catherine of Alexandria. Since 1975 the sanctuary has been entrusted to a small group of lay brothers led by a Benedictine monk.

After your tour of the convent catch the next ferry back to Stresa.

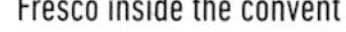

Food and Drink

① Casa della Neve

Loc. Mottarone; www.casadellaneve.it

This family-run hotel restaurant enjoys great vistas of the Monte Rosa chain. Many of the specialities are geared to warm up winter skiers: fondues, pork ragout, jugged deer. Lighter fare in summer. €

The Monte Rosa Massif mountain range

Fresco inside the convent

TOUR 4
Villa Taranto and Lake Mergozzo

Take an enjoyable and scenic stroll to Villa Taranto and admire the most famous gardens of Lake Maggiore. Walk along Pallanza's fashionable promenade, then discover the charm of tiny Lake Mergozzo and its enchanting fishing village.

DISTANCE: Ferry: 6km (3.75 miles), walk: 4km (2.5 miles), bus/taxi: 8km (5 miles)
TIME: A half day or leisurely full day
START: Stresa
END: Mergozzo
POINTS TO NOTE: Ferries to Villa Taranto (45 mins) are more direct but less frequent than those to Pallanza (about 35 mins and a short walk to the villa). Allow at least an hour, but preferably two (or more) for Villa Taranto. If you want to hire a bike or take a bus or taxi from Pallanza to Mergozzo, ask for advice at Pallanza's tourist office at Via S. Bernardino, 49 (www.viviverbania.it). A quick way back to Stresa from Mergozzo via public transport is a direct train (www.trenitalia.com).

From the jetty on Stresa's Piazza Marconi take a morning ferry to Villa Taranto (or to Pallanza, see Points to Note). If you want to have a picnic lunch, buy provisions from Carrefour at Via Roma 11, in Stresa, before you leave. (An area near the entrance of Villa Taranto is allocated to picnickers; alternatively, you could plan to picnic on a beach at Lake Mergozzo.) Most of the boats call en route at **Baveno**, set in the lee of a pink granite mountain. A small, subdued version of Stresa, the resort prospered from quarried pink granite and has been popular with British visitors since Victorian times.

Villa Taranto

Pallanza has some fine gardens, but none of them matches those of **Villa Taranto** ❶ (www.villataranto.it; charge). The landing stage, right in front of the entrance, was created specifically for the gardens when they opened in 1952.

The garden

In 1931 Neil McEacharn, a retired Scottish soldier and passionate horticulturist, saw an advertisement in *The Times* for the estate known

Prized tulips at Villa Taronto

as La Crocetta on a hillside in Pallanza. He bought the property and devoted the rest of his life to planting and landscaping the site. What had formerly been an unruly wooded headland was transformed into one of Europe's leading botanical gardens. McEacharn imported plants from five different continents – most notably from Asia. Among them were exotic plants, such as coffee, tea, cotton, lotus blossom, giant Amazonian water lilies and papyrus.

The gardens have more than 20,000 plant species and are equally lovely in spring and autumn. Tulip-lined flower beds contrast with exotic aquatic plants; there is also a wooded ravine and a soothing water garden with fountains and ponds. In April and May, cherry blossom floats over violets, narcissi and crocuses, and camellias, azaleas, irises and rhododendrons also all flourish. From 25 April to May every year there are 80,000 bulbs in flower at Villa Taranto. The star is the tulip – over 65 varieties are planted. During the week one ticket out of every five sold at Villa Taranto has a stamp on the back entitling the visitor to a free plant or flower cultivated in the garden.

Summer is the time to see aquatic plants, oleanders, hydrangeas, roses and citrus fruits; autumn for coppery Japanese maples, flowering shrubs and mellow dahlias.

Don't miss the giant water lilies in the Victoria Amazonica Greenhouse. They measure up to 2m (6.5ft), with leaves that look like huge green trays. The flowers, which are nocturnal and pollinated by beetles, only live for around 24 hours, and gradually change colour from creamy white to pink and purplish red.

Since McEacharn left the villa to the state, Villa Taranto has been a venue for political summits (held in the villa itself, which is closed to the public), each marked by a tree-planting ceremony. Trees have been planted here by various heads of state, including Margaret Thatcher.

Giant water lilies

Perfect symmetry in the gardens

Pallanza

Leave the gardens and follow the Via Vittorio Veneto, the lakeside road, for about thirty minutes on foot around the headland to Corso Zanitello in **Pallanza ❷**, where magnolia and oleander trees line the quaysides and colourful cafés flank the piazzas.

During the medieval era Pallanza was protected by a castle and was the only town on the lake not to fall under Borromean sway. The resort's mild winter climate, fine views and luxuriant gardens attract the elderly during off-season, while a smattering of bars and clubs in medieval Pallanza draw younger visitors in summer.

Villa Giulia

Villa Giulia is a frothy pink concoction built in 1847 originally owned by Bernardino Branca, inventor of Fernet Branca, and now serving as a convention and concert venue. The gardens are a public park and command views of the private islet of San Giovanni, which the conductor Toscanini acquired from the Borromean family.

Eating options

If you are ready for refreshment at this point, allow yourself to be tempted by the exquisitely elegant lakeside **Ristorante Milano** overlooking the picturesque old harbour, see ①.

Suna

The garden-lined lakeside promenade continues for another 2km (1.25 miles). At the far side of the resort, you can watch the watersports around **Suna**. This former fishing village buzzes with beach life, although the occasional villa and Romanesque church hark back to a quieter era. If you are contemplating a meal now or later for a buffet *aperitivo* or dinner, the **Hostaria Dam a Traa**, see ②, is a relaxed restaurant with a terrace overlooking the lake.

Fondotoce Nature Reserve

Towards the end of Via Troubetskoy, the promenade merges into the busy coastal road. The 360ha (890-acre) **Riserva Naturale Fondotoce** protects the wetlands to the west, habitat of numerous species of waterfowl and other marsh bird

Colourful Pallanza

Food and Drink

1 Ristorante Milano
Corso Zanitello 2/4, Pallanza; www.ristorantemilanolagomaggiore.IT
Frighteningly pricey, but it is worth splashing out for the romantic lakeside location, the exquisite fish dishes and the succulent meat from Piedmont. Needless to say, the food is freshly sourced, the setting elegant and the service faultless. €€€€

2 Hostaria Dam a Traa
Via Paolo Troubetzkoy 106, Suna; www.damatraa.it
Wrap yourself in a warm and relaxing atmosphere and discover traditional flavours with an elegant and modern twist. The menu offers typical à la carte dishes as well as dishes of the day. Vegetarian friendly; gluten-free options available. €€€

3 La Quartina
Hotel La Quartina, Via Pallanza 22, Lago di Mergozzo; www.laquartina.com
Hugging the shore of Lake Mergozzo, this relaxing hotel-restaurant serves fish from the lake, local salamis and cheese along with Piemontese beef and game from the hills. €€

but the area around Fondotoce is somewhat spoilt by campsites.

Lake Mergozzo

By bus or taxi it is about 10km (6 miles) northwest from Pallanza to the village of **Mergozzo** ❸. Framed by enchanting forests, tiny **Lago di Mergozzo** is one of the cleanest lakes in Europe (motorboats are banned) and the beaches are secluded. Prior to the 9th century it was part of Lake Maggiore, but silt from the River Toce separated it from the larger lake.

Once you arrive at the village of Mergozzo, the lakeside restaurant of **Hotel Due Palme** near to the main piazza, makes for another nice place to pause before exploring the picturesque hamlet as it curves around the fishing harbour; inviting alleys and flights of steps lead to a cloistered church and old-fashioned inns.

Alternatively, sample one of the tasting menus at **La Quartina**, see 3, or try the gastronomic delights of the two-Michelin star **Il Piccolo Lago** (see page 115), but note the opening times.

From Mergozzo catch a bus to Intra/Verbania. Then take the ferry back to Stresa where you can enjoy an *aperitivo* as the sun sets, offering a perfect moment to reflect on your day.

The rooftops of Mergozzo

Lake Mergozzo

TOUR 5
Lake Maggiore Express

A combination of lake cruises and mountain railway, crossing from Italy into Switzerland, this tour offers some of the most sensational scenery in Northern Europe. A three-hour ferry trip is followed by a narrow-gauge railway ride through the Ticino mountains.

DISTANCE: Ferry: 61km (38 miles), train: 96km (60 miles)
TIME: A full day, possibly two
START: Stresa ferry landing stage
END: Stresa railway station
POINTS TO NOTE: Tickets include a lake cruise and rail journey. Book in advance, especially in high season. Contact www.vigezzinacentovalli.com/esperienze/lago-maggiore-express.html. Passports are essential. A two-day ticket allows more time to explore the upper lake and mountain villages and includes a free lake pass. Operates daily except Wed. Mid-April to mid-October.

Begin your tour from any ferry stop on Lake Maggiore, taking the cruise north to Locarno in Switzerland.

Stresa to the Upper Lake

From Stresa, the triple-decker *battello* ferry skirts the **Borromean Islands** and then stops at the resort of **Baveno** ❶ (see page 40). The next stop is **Pallanza** ❷ (see page 42), where grandiose villas and a garden-lined promenade overlook the lake. From neighbouring Intra, the boat crosses to Laveno on the eastern side of the lake.

Upper Lake Maggiore

The main resorts of the northern lake lie on the sunny western shores. **Cannero Riviera** ❸ occupies a charming site amid subtropical flora, looking over to picturesque islets with ruins of the Malpaga castles. Dating from the 12th century, the castles belonged to the five Mazzarditi brothers, brigands who plundered local villages. The Visconti destroyed their strongholds in 1414, then a century later, the Borromeo family built fortifications here – the remains of which you see today. **Cannobio** ❹, the last town before the Swiss border, has steep medieval streets behind a long promenade of pastel-washed façades. If you are on a two-day ticket, this is definitely a place to explore.

Lake Maggiore Express in the Centovalli valley

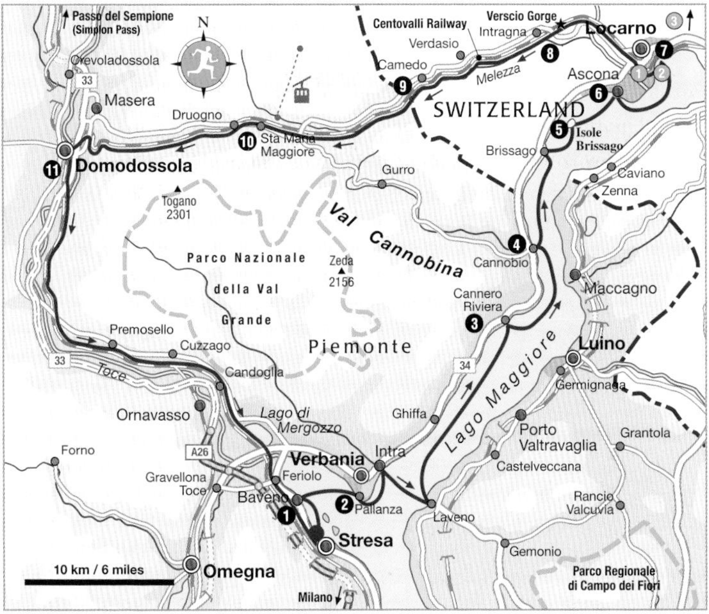

North into Switzerland

Across the Swiss border, the first stop is Brissago, which is noticeably more modern than the nearby Italian villages. The larger of the two **Isole Brissago** ❺ (Brissago Islands) is home to the **Parco Botanico del Cantone Ticino**, created in 1883 by Baroness Antoinette de Saint-Léger and full of exotic flora. She set up residence here and inspired artists, writers and musicians to visit the island.

Ascona

The boat heads on to the little resort of **Ascona** ❻, where multicoloured houses line the waterfront. Paul Klee, Hermann Hesse and Isadora Duncan were among those lured by its charms.

Locarno

Over the river from Ascona lies **Locarno** ❼, a southwest-facing town with a mild climate and flourishing parks and gardens. Pick up a map when you disembark, or turn left for the tourist office, and locate the nearby station where you will take the train to Domodossola. On a day trip you are likely to have between 1.5–3.5 hours in Locarno, depending

Crossing the border

A fifth of Lake Maggiore lies in Switzerland, in the Italian-speaking canton of Ticino. The resorts are Italian in feel, with their bright piazzas and alfresco eateries, but there is a marked Swiss efficiency about them: while the Italian lakeside villages retain their ancient patina, façades in Switzerland look as though they were painted yesterday. You may be tempted by the stylish shops in Locarno; if so, remember that the local currency is Swiss francs, and although euros are accepted here, you will usually receive change in Swiss francs – often at a poor exchange rate.

on which train you opt for. The 52km (32.5-mile) railway line from Locarno to Domodossola opened in 1923. Until recently, passengers travelled in vintage carriages with wooden interiors – more romantic but less comfortable than today's electric trains.

The heart of Locarno is the porticoed **Piazza Grande**, just back from the lakefront, where you can sit at cafés and people-watch. In summer, this is the venue for open-air concerts, and in August, it hosts the International Film Festival. From the piazza, follow the lanes running west of the square for the **Città Vecchia** (Old Town) and Via Cittadella, where **La Cittadella**, see ①, serves excellent pizzas and fish.

Refreshment

You may arrive in Locarno too late to lunch in some of the restaurants, but many cafés and pizzerias open all day. The most inviting spots are Piazza Grande or lakeside Viale Verbano, where **Al Pozz**, see ②, is open all day for full meals, as is neighbouring **Centenario** (see page 115).

Sanctuary of Madonna del Sasso

For stunning views of the lake and Alps, take the **funicular** (www.funicolarelocarno.ch; 200m/yds northwest of the landing stage, daily starting from around 8am, with the last service in the late afternoon or evening – exact timings depending on the month; charge) that climbs up the hill every 15 or 30 minutes (depending on the season), or walk up the pathway flanked by chapels to the **Santuario della Madonna del Sasso**, a Capuchin monastery founded in 1480. Here, the **Ristorante Funicolare**, see ③, is a great spot to admire the view.

Centovalli and Valle Vigezzo

The Centovalli trains depart from below Locarno's **railway station** (Via della Stazione), which is 200m/yds north of the landing stage. Follow directions for Funivia Locarno–Domodossola, and when you board

The sanctuary of Madonna del Sasso

Food and Drink

1 La Cittadella
Via Cittadella 18, Locarno, www.cittadella.ch
Downstairs is an informal pizzeria, while upstairs is a smart seafood restaurant; the food at both is delicious. Booking advised. €€

2 Al Pozz
Viale Verbano 21, Locarno, www.alpozz.ch
Open all day for pizzas and Mediterranean cuisine, Al Pozz has great views of Lake Maggiore and the mountains from its terrace. *Pollo nel cestello* (chicken in a basket) and spaghetti clams are specialities. €€

3 Ristorante Funicolare
Via Santuario 4, Orselina, Locarno, www.ristorantefunicolare.ch
Perched above Locarno, at the top of the Sanctuary of Madonna del Sasso, this is worth a trip for the views alone. The menu is likely to feature *lake fish*, as well as meat and pasta and vegetarian dishes. The outdoor barbequed fish is particularly good. Alternatively, just go for coffee and cake. €€

the train, secure a seat on the near side for the best views. Once you have emerged from the tunnel, you will be travelling through a wild, spectacular region; the little train snakes its way slowly around steep, wooded valleys, passing waterfalls and crossing precarious-looking bridges and viaducts above dramatic gorges. Deepest of all is the gorge of Verscio, a haven for bungee-jumpers.

Mountain hamlets

The railway follows the course of the River Melezza, stopping at neat mountain hamlets, with their chalet-style houses and lofty steeples. **Intragna** 8 has a lovely 16th-century bridge, as well as a viaduct (another spot for bungee-jumping). (If you are on the two-day trip, you can take a cable-car up to Costa and Pila from here.)

After a customs-check at **Camedo** 9 on the border, you are back in Italy. From here, the train climbs up to **Santa Maria Maggiore** 10, which, at 830m (2,723ft), is the highest point of the journey. The village is home to a several art galleries.

Domodossola to Stresa

The trip ends at **Domodossola** 11, not far from the Simplon Pass. From here you should transfer to the normal Trenitalia rail service for Stresa. The final lap of the journey takes just half an hour.

An interior detail of the sanctuary

Colourful Ascona

TOUR 6
Lake Orta

For all its popularity with Italians and foreigners alike, Lake Orta has managed to retain a certain mystique. This driving tour will transport you to a dreamy pocket of Piedmont, the highlights of which are the medieval village of Orta San Giulio and the Isola San Giulio in the centre of the lake.

DISTANCE: 85km (53 miles), returning via Gravellona Toce
TIME: A full day
START/END: Stresa
POINTS TO NOTE: Avoid Orta on Sundays when coachloads of visitors descend on the village. If you are thinking of a meal at Villa Crespi (see page 116), be sure to reserve. Note that the village of Orta San Giulio is closed to traffic during the season, and cars must be left in the paying parking lots above the centre.

Separated from Lake Maggiore by the Mottarone peak, Orta is the westernmost of the lakes. Just 14km (9 miles) long and 3km (2 miles) wide, it is tiny in comparison to lakes Maggiore, Como or Garda. It is not so much the scenery that makes it unmissable, but the village of Orta San Giulio and the picturesque little Isola San Giulio.

Between lakes Maggiore and Orta, the Mottarone peak commands a wonderful panorama of the lakes and Alps. A road leads up there from Gignese but be warned: you will have to pay several euros to get there, as the last section is a toll road owned by the omnipotent Borromeo family. You can also access the peak on foot.

Gignese

Leaving Stresa by car, follow the signs for Gignese and climb the Mottarone. After 8km (5 miles), you will reach the hill village of **Gignese ❶**, best-known for the **Museo dell'Ombrello e del Parasole** (Umbrella and Parasol Museum; www.gignese.it/museo; charge), a large collection of fanciful umbrellas, dating to 1850. Continue to Armeno and descend southwest towards Lake Orta and Orta San Giulio.

Sacro Monte

Take the main approach road, which passes the entrance to the **Sacro Monte ❷** (Holy Mount; www.sacrimonti.org/en/sacro-monte-di-orta; opening times

Orta San Giulio at dusk

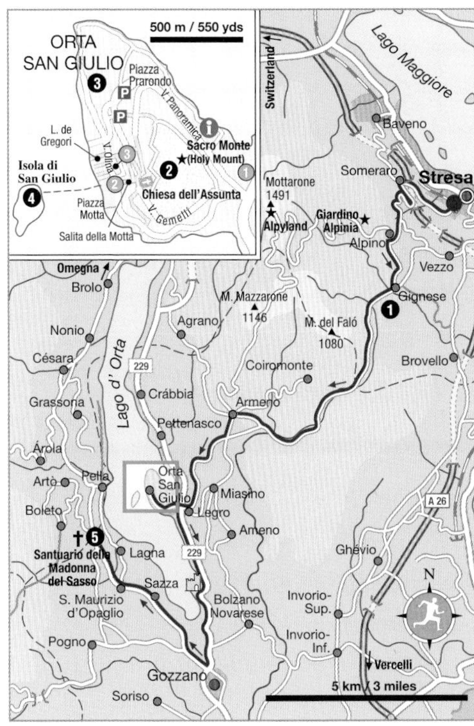

climax of Franciscan devotional routes that evoke the symbolic journey through the Holy Land. Set on a wooded hillside, Orta's route wends through a series of twenty frescoed chapels, with some 400 life-size terracotta statues that trace the history of St Francis. Slate-roofed Renaissance and Baroque chapels are full of devotional paintings and statues by Lombard artists. The route is well worth following for its peaceful atmosphere and misty views. A stop at **AgriGelateria** is a great way to start or finish your walk, see ①.

Orta San Giulio

Set snugly on a peninsula, **Orta San Giulio** ❸ has long been a fashionable if discreet resort, known for its chic hotels as much as for its soft light and air of spirituality. Take the atmospheric Via Gemelli from the Sacro Monte to the village. You will emerge outside the Baroque **Chiesa dell'Assunta** (Church of the Assumption), host of a spring concert festival complete with full historical pageantry. The church commands a dramatic view of the sloping

for the church and grounds vary; free). Leave your car in the higher of the two car parks, which is conveniently situated for access to the pedestrianised historic centre of Orta San Giulio.

Sacri Monti are prominent features of this corner of the lakes, and Orta's is the finest, rivalled only by the one in Varese (see page 54). Linked to tiny chapels, the Sacri Monti are the

Colourful façades, Orta San Giulio

Sacro Monte fresco

Salita della Motta, which winds down to the main square, passing geranium-bedecked balconies and Renaissance palaces with peach-coloured façades.

Piazza Motta

The descent ends at **Piazza Motta** by the quaint waterfront. The piazza is lined with outdoor cafés and old-fashioned hotels, including the **Leon d'Oro**, which has a good restaurant, see 2. The hub of village life, Piazza Motta is particularly animated during the Wednesday market.

Overlooking the square is the arcaded former town hall, the **Palazzo della Comunità**, frescoes of which feature a serpent symbol relating to Orta's mythical origins. This façade is an exception in the town – buildings here tend to be painted in muted shades of ochre, green or pink; white is forbidden.

Take **Via Olina**, the main thoroughfare, if you want to indulge in some idle window-shopping in the medieval quarter, and perhaps book a table at the **Olina** restaurant in the Piccolo Hotel, see 3.

Not far away, on Largo de Gregori, you will find **Salumeria Rovera**, a whimsical salami shop that features somewhat alarming paintings of piglets tucking into a pork feast.

Isola di San Giulio

At Orta San Giulio's picturesque jetty, friendly boatmen guide ferries and motorboats to the **Isola di San Giulio** 4, a tiny haven of tranquillity and supplication. In the convent (closed to the public) at the heart of the isle, blue-robed Benedictine nuns devote themselves to contemplation, work and prayer.

Chattering visitors clambering out of boats beside the **Basilica di San Giulio** are soon hushed by the sombre mood of this Romanesque church. The island was supposedly overrun by serpents and dragons until AD390, when Julius, a Christian preacher, succeeded in banishing them, before erecting a basilica in celebration. Fragments of the 5th-century church are visible in the crypt.

Spiritual injunctions

The circular **Via Giulino**, which hugs the high walls of the nunnery, carries injunctions to follow the right path. In a bid to evoke 'the island within', there are two pilgrimage paths: the Way of Meditation and the Way of Silence. The island forsakes its silence only in June, when a festival of ancient music is staged.

Sanctuary of Madonna del Sasso

After Orta San Giulio, the other towns on the lake come as something of an anticlimax. Nevertheless, if you have time, it is worth taking the short drive to the sanctuary that overlooks the lake.

From Orta San Giulio, head south along the shore towards Gozzano

The magical Isola di San Giulio

Food and Drink

1 AgriGelateria
Via Domodossola 5, Orta San Giulio, 53 434 2866
A perfect spot to beat the heat either before or after your walk to the Sacro. Kids and adults will enjoy the numerous and delicious flavours. Connected to the ice cream shop is a small pizzeria in case you need a little more sustenance. €

2 Leon d'Oro
Piazza Motta 42, Orta San Giulio, www.albergoleondoro.it
An idyllic location with a long shady terrace overlooking Isola San Giulio and a tempting menu of local dishes, including risotto, homemade pasta, fresh lake fish and wonderful puddings. €€€

3 Olina
Via Olina 40, Orta San Giulio, 0322 905656
Make the most of the complimentary *aperitivo* then tuck into artfully presented local specialities, including vegetarian dishes. €€

and follow the western shore to San Maurizio d'Opaglio, an area known as 'tap country' due to the presence of Italy's finest tap- and bath-makers. While these manufacturers prospered on orders from Arab sheikhs, Lake Orta suffered pollution from industrial waste. However, in the early 1990s a cleaning programme coincided with a collapse of the gold-tap market, resulting in waters fit for swimming once more.

Resist the Tap Museum in San Maurizio d'Opaglio in favour of the **Santuario della Madonna del Sasso** **5** (www.santuariomadonnadelsasso.it; free), which is just 2km (1.25 miles) away, above Pella. Clearly signposted, it is at the heart of a pleasant series of hamlets. The Baroque frescoed church, built on a granite outcrop over the lake, has fine views over mountains and lake.

Return to Stresa

You can return to Lake Maggiore by continuing along the western shore, passing Pella, Nonio and Omegna, then heading north to Gravellona Toce and returning to Stresa via Baveno. Or return the way you came, through Gignese, dining perhaps at Orta San Giulio before heading back to Stresa.

Villa Crespi

If you have a taste for the exotic this is where you will find the **Villa Crespi** (see pages 106 and 116), a fairytale Moorish fantasy erected in 1879 by a local cotton merchant inspired by his travels to Baghdad and Persia. The villa is situated out of the medieval centre, at the entrance to the town, so parking is easy.

TOUR 7

Varese and Lake Lugano

A full-day country and lakeside drive from Varese, nudging the Swiss border on Lake Lugano. A tour of Villa Panza's contemporary art collection is followed by a visit to Varese's nature reserve, then lunch in Luino on Lake Maggiore and a scenic drive along the shores of Lake Lugano.

DISTANCE: 85km (53 miles)
TIME: A full day
START/END: Varese
POINTS TO NOTE: Note that Villa Cicogna-Mozzoni is open only on Sundays and national holidays from April to October. Another option is to make this day trip on a Wednesday when Luino holds its market Il Mercato di Luino (until 5pm); one of the biggest in Italy, it sells food, clothes, leather, textiles, household goods, etc. It is a good idea to bring your passport in case you are tempted to visit Switzerland.

Varese

Begin in the city of **Varese**. Essentially a modern industrial city, Varese has styled itself as a *Città Giardino*, or Garden City. It also has a small historic centre, as well as sophisticated shopping – it is Italy's shoe-making capital.

Villa Panza

Varese's top cultural attraction is Villa Panza, which houses a major collection of modern American art. From the centre of Varese head north along Via Veratti, which becomes Viale Aguggiari. **Villa Panza** ❶ (www.fondoambiente.it; last entry 45 mins before closing; may be closed on holidays; charge) is signposted to the right after about 1km (0.75 mile) from the city centre. Count Giuseppe Panza, the last owner of this frescoed 18th-century mansion, donated it to the nation in 1996. The interior is enhanced by an outstanding collection of abstract American art dating from the 1950s and strong on work from the 1980s and 1990s.

Classical versus contemporary

Rather than disperse his eclectic collection among his five sons, Panza left it to the Fondo per l'Ambiente Italiano (FAI), the Italian equivalent of the National Trust. As both a listed monument and an art gallery, the villa appeals to both lovers of contemporary

Sacro Monte di Varese in winter

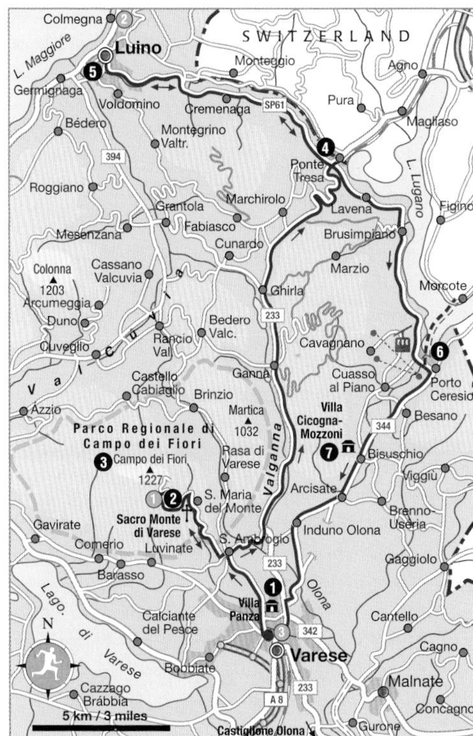

art and fans of classical architecture. The former will appreciate the abstract tonal canvases, rooms bathed in brash neon light, bizarre installations and ceilings exposed to the elements. Classicists will admire the old Tuscan chests, Empire-style dining room and magnificent ballroom hung with chandeliers and subdued abstracts. There is also a fine collection of African and pre-Columbian art.

Lake Varese

Shaped like a battered boot, Lago di Varese is a small lake lying west of Varese. It is a gentle, unremarkable lake framed by rolling hills. From Biandronno on the western shore, you can cross to a tiny, wooded island, Isolino Virginia, which has a restaurant and the remains of prehistoric pile-dwellings.

Sacro Monte di Varese

If the weather allows, consider making a short visit to the Sacro Monte di Varese (Holy Mount of Varese) and the Parco Regionale di Campo dei Fiori. From Villa Panza return to Viale Arguggiari and head north along the same road for about 6km (3.75 miles), following the signs to Sacro Monte and Campo dei Fiori. A winding road climbs through the heart of Varese's villa zone, where the hills are dotted with *belle époque* and Art Nouveau concoctions perched on grassy knolls.

Farmer's market in Varese

Varese, 'City of Gardens'

The **Sacro Monte di Varese** ❷ is a major pilgrimage site on the wooded slopes of Monte Campo dei Fiori. Along the steep Via Sacra are fourteen devotional shrines with life-size terracotta figures and frescoes. From the **Santuario di Santa Maria del Monte**, and its village at the top, there are vertiginous views down over Lake Varese.

If you are in need of refreshment, stop for a drink and snack on the terrace of the **Al Borducan Ristorante Romantico** (as long as you don't have children with you) see ①, near the **Sacro Monte**.

Campo dei Fiori Regional Park

Continue another 5km (3 miles) beyond Santa Maria del Monte to the **Parco Regionale di Campo dei Fiori** ❸ (www.parcocampodeifiori.it; free) with six nature reserves and sixteen marked trails. Almost at the top of the Campo dei Fiori mountain (1,226m/4,022ft) sits the G.V. Schiaparelli astronomical observatory, conceived by Salvatore Furia, who defused and detonated thousands of unexploded mines to build the road to the reserve.

Lake Lugano

From the park, retrace your route, pass the Sacro Monte and take the first road on the left to join the SS233 to **Ponte Tresa** ❹ on Lake Lugano (27km/16.75 miles). The lake, which zigzags across the Swiss border, is wilder and less majestic than Lake Maggiore. Just over a third of the shoreline belongs to Italy, the rest to the Italian-speaking Swiss canton of Ticino. Steep wooded mountains rising sheer from the water preclude development along most of the shoreline. Lugano is the only large town.

Ponte Tresa is a steamer stop and border village, packed at rush hour with Italian commuters travelling to and from Lugano. More peaceful and picturesque is the village of **Lavena**, set on a headland a couple of kilometres (1.25 miles) to the southeast.

Lunch in Luino

From Ponte Tresa, head west on the SP61 to **Luino** ❺ on Lake Maggiore. You could stop here for a lakeside stroll and lunch, or take the lakeshore road 2km (1.25 miles) north to Colmegna for lunch at the **Relais Villa Porta** see ②. Encircled by woods, Luino was once a centre for smugglers, whose contraband coffee and cigarettes would pass between Switzerland and Italy as market forces dictated.

Porto Ceresio

After lunch head back to Ponte Tresa and follow the shore of Lake Lugano as far as **Porto Ceresio** ❻ (10km/6.25 miles), one of the most scenic drives in the province of Varese. A pretty Italian outpost, Porto Ceresio centres on an elegant harbour framed by steep shores. The name Porto Ceresio comes from the Latin name for Lake Lugano – Ceresio – which is still used by Italians.

If time permits, consider a ferry crossing from the Italian port to its Swiss

Lake Lugano

Food and Drink

1 Al Borducan Ristorante Romantico
Hotel Borducan, Via Beata Caterina Moriggi 43, www.ristorante borducan.com
In an atmospheric Art Nouveau hotel restricted to couples only, this restaurant is famous for the Elixir Al Borducan that is also used to enhance historic recipes. Food is prepared according to the Bregonzio family tradition. Cuisine is inspired by seasonal ingredients, scents, and spices. From their terrace you can enjoy the view of the lakes as well as the massif of Campo dei Fiori, and a private garden. €€€

2 Relais Villa Porta
Via A. Palazzi 1, Colmegna (2km/1.25 miles north of Luino), www.relaisvillaporta.com
The hotel's two terraces overlook Lake Maggiore, which provides the ingredients for dishes such as carp in sweet and sour sauce and perch with tagliatelle. The villa was built in the early 18th century as part of a hunting estate and retains a large park with trails and a waterfall. €€€€

3 Hotel Bologna
Via Broggi 7, Varese, www.albergobologna.it
This popular hotel restaurant in Varese's historic centre offers hearty helpings of hams and salamis, fresh pastas, steaks, fish and creamy desserts. Booking essential. €€

rival across the water. The picturesque village of **Morcote** is set on the tip of the peninsula that runs down the lake towards Italy. Known as the 'pearl of Lake Lugano', it has a maze of alleys and is dominated by a medieval church.

Villa Cicogna-Mozzoni

From Porto Ceresio, take the SS344 south to Varese, stopping after 5km (3 miles) at Bisuschio to visit **Villa Cicogna-Mozzoni** 7 (www.villacicognamozzoni.it; charge), an impressive Renaissance stately home inhabited by the genial Count Cicogna-Mozzoni.

The family fortunes were founded on a happy accident: in 1476 Galeazzo Sforza, the powerful duke of Milan, was out hunting when he chanced upon a bear on the rampage. He was saved from certain death by Agostino Mozzoni and his dog. To express his gratitude, the duke of Milan funded a scheme to transform Mozzoni's simple hunting lodge into this lovely villa, complete with Italianate gardens, formal box hedges and fountains.

Dinner options

If you are heading back to Varese, opt for the restaurant of the **Hotel Bologna**, see 3.

Campo dei Fiori in autumn

Sophisticated Porto Ceresio

TOUR 8
Villa Carlotta and Bellagio

Spend the morning exploring Villa Carlotta's gardens at Tremezzo, then catch a ferry to Bellagio, the 'pearl' of Lake Como, where you can wander the town's cobbled alleys and stroll in the grounds of Villa Serbelloni or Villa Melzi.

DISTANCE: Tremezzo to Bellagio by ferry: 3km/2 miles; walking in Bellagio: 2–4km (1.25–2.5 miles), depending on sites covered
TIME: A full day
START: Villa Carlotta
END: Bellagio
POINTS TO NOTE: If you are travelling to Villa Carlotta from Como (35km/22miles) allow forty minutes by hydrofoil or about ninety mins by ferry. The last hydrofoil back to Como from Bellagio leaves at around 8pm, earlier off-season. Bellagio is packed with restaurants, but you could also consider a picnic in the gardens of Villa Carlotta (there are two allocated picnic areas).

Central Lake Como

The inspiration of writers, artists and composers, **Lake Como** is the most romantic of the three main Italian lakes. It has long been famed for its natural beauty, fine panoramas and sumptuous villas and gardens. The lake is shaped like an inverted Y, caused by the division of an ancient glacier that carved out its valley. The three branches of the lake converge at the Punta Spartivento (the 'Point that divides the Wind'), the setting of famous Bellagio, 'pearl of the lake'.

Henry James was well aware of Lake Como's reputation for illicit trysts: 'It is commonly the spot to which inflamed young gentlemen invite the wives of other gentlemen to fly with them and ignore the restrictions of public opinion.' It was here, according to locals, that President Kennedy romanced Marilyn Monroe.

Villa Carlotta

Villa Carlotta ❶ (www.villacarlotta.it; charge) has its own landing stage, but you can also access it via Tremezzo (450m/yds to the south) or Cadenabbia (1km/0.6 mile to the north), which has a car-ferry service.

Graced by magnificent gardens, the villa was a wedding present from a Prussian princess to her daughter, Princess Carlotta of Nassau. Carlotta established

Canova's 'Cupid and Psyche'

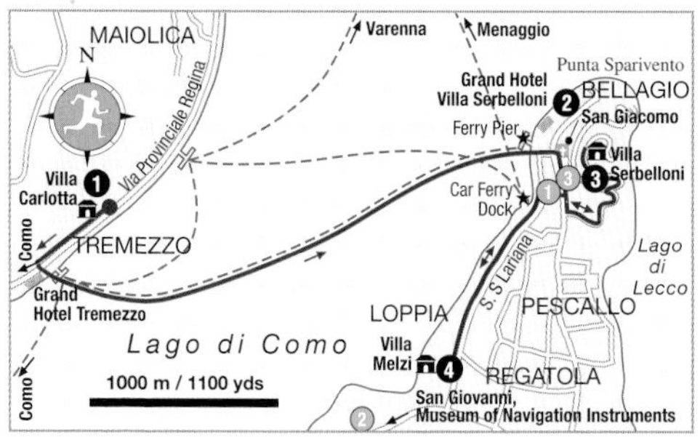

Zealand, eucalyptus and succulents from Australia and giant sequoias from South America.

a small court here and completed the landscaping of the gardens in the 1860s. As a result, guests are greeted by a prosperous Baroque pile, bordered by a profusion of pink and white azaleas and a theatrical staircase that leads up to orange and lemon terraces.

Highlights

The villa inevitably plays second fiddle to the gardens; its large formal rooms contain a mixed collection of paintings and Neoclassical statuary by Canova, including the *Cupid and Psyche*, symbol of the villa and a copy of the original in the Louvre.

Allow plenty of time for the gardens. There are 5.6ha (14 acres) and over 500 species of trees and shrubs, including 150 different varieties of azaleas and rhododendrons. The plants evoke an exotic map of the world: cedars of Lebanon, Egyptian papyrus, Japanese maples and banana trees, Chinese bamboo, Indian tea, Mediterranean agaves, ferns from New

Tremezzo

A short walk south is the resort of **Tremezzo**. While its heyday was in the 1930s, any thoughts of living on past laurels have been banished since the sophisticated restyling of a very old lady indeed – the Grand Hotel Tremezzo.

Bellagio

From Tremezzo, frequent steamers cross the lake to **Bellagio** ❷. Walks around this cape afford sublime views of mountains in all directions, most notably north to the often-snow-capped mountains along the Swiss border.

Keen walkers and hikers seeking inspiration for trails should look at www.mylakecomo.co. Also useful is the international site www.alltrails.com, which will send routes direct to your phone. Other outdoor activities include rock-climbing and watersports.

On Bellagio's bustling waterfront, houses lead to a promenade lined with oleanders and limes. There are red-roofed houses, pastel-tinged façades, steep cobbled alleys, quaint craft shops, a Romanesque belltower and lakeside vistas.

Fresco detail, Villa Carlotta

Graceful Tremezzo

Shopping along Salita Mella

To explore one of the prettiest alleys, take the steep **Salita Mella**, just opposite the passenger landing stage. There are some enticing boutiques here, such as Pierangelo Masciadri's shop, Arte e Moda, at No. 19, where you can buy beautiful scarves and ties with designs inspired by classical mythology, Renaissance paintings and rationalist architecture. Bill Clinton, George W. Bush and Bill Gates are among those who have commissioned ties from Pierangelo – he has thank-you letters to prove it.

Just before Pierangelo's shop, on the left at No. 18, is **La Barchetta**, see 1, a good choice for regional cuisine if it is time for lunch.

Climb to the top of the street for Via G. Garibaldi, the main shopping street with leather and silk to suit all budgets and some very tempting delis. The road leads to Piazza della Chiesa with the much-restored Romanesque Church of San Giacomo and a tower that is all that is left of Bellagio's medieval defence system.

Villa Serbelloni

For the best views from Bellagio, join an afternoon tour of the gardens of **Villa Serbelloni** 3 (guided tours only with a minimum of six people and weather permitting; tours start from the medieval tower in Piazza della Chiesa; tickets online www.villagiolakecomo.com; charge). Not to be confused with the exclusive hotel of the same name on the lake, the villa itself belongs to the Rockefeller Foundation and is not open to the public. The steep and winding path takes you high above Bellagio, through fine gardens, for stunning panoramas of both sides of the promontory.

Villa Melzi

Having explored some of the steep alleys, return to the lake. You can't get lost – all the alleys lead down to the waterfront. Turn left at the lake for a gentle lakeside promenade, passing Bellagio's renovated lido (www.lidodibellagio.com), to **Villa Melzi** 4 (Lungolario Manzoni; www.giardinidivillamelzi.it; charge), an austere Neoclassical villa set in the first 'English' gardens on the lake.

Although the villa is a private residence and closed to the public, the romantic grounds enchant visitors. Beyond the entrance, Japanese water gardens are cleverly concealed from the lake, and an intimate mood is created by an ornamental pool, framed by cedars, maples, camphor and myrrh. On the grassy banks beyond, rhododendrons and camellias create a blaze of colour in spring. Below, standing guard by the lake, is a quaint gazebo that captivated Stendhal and Liszt. Beside this bold folly, an avenue of plane trees leads along the shore to the small history museum in the orangerie, the villa, family chapel and Loppia landing stage.

Lakeside dining on Como

Food and Drink

① La Barchetta

Salita Mella, Bellagio 15; www.ristorantebarchetta.com

Long-established lake fish and seafood restaurant situated up one of the steep, narrow alleys from the waterfront. You won't get the lakeside views, but there is a heated bamboo-covered terrace, service is friendly, and the food (creative pastas, creamy risottos and delicious fresh fish) is a cut above the average eatery on the lake. They also serve pizza and other simple dishes downstairs and on the pavement in the more casual Ristoro Forma & Gusto. €€

② Silvio

Via Carcano 10–12, Bellagio, www.bellagiosilvio.com

This inviting modern fish restaurant above the gardens of Villa Melzi has wonderful lake views. It serves some of the freshest lake fish in Bellagio, caught by the family who run the restaurant. Reasonably priced rooms are also available. €€

③ Bilacus

Salita Serbelloni 32, Bellagio, www.bilacusbellagio.it

No lake views here but there is a delightful arbour for alfresco meals. This family-run restaurant offers attentive, friendly service and inventive, beautifully presented dishes such as risotto with borage, goats' cheese and scallop or guinea fowl with almonds. €€

Eating options

For lunch or dinner, avoid the waterfront tourist traps in favour of the fish restaurant, **Silvio**, see ②, a short walk from Villa Melzi, or **Bilacus** see ③, up from the waterfront. If you fancy an extravagant dinner on a luxury hotel's lakeside terrace, or perhaps a cocktail in one of its bars, before a water-taxi ride home to reality, consider **Mistral** in the Grand Hotel Villa Serbelloni (see page 117). Otherwise, wait for a ferry in Bar Sanremo on the waterfront.

San Giovanni

In the hamlet of San Giovanni, the Museum of Navigation Instruments (Piazza Don Miotti; www.bellagiomuseo.com; charge) displays over two hundred marine-themed exhibits, including antique sundials, compasses and 18th-century Venetian telescopes, many of them beautiful, even if navigational instruments do not usually raise your heartbeat. The museum is about half an hour on foot in the Villa Melzi direction; alternatively, take the tourist train that departs from the ferry station and does a circuit of the peninsula.

The pastel-hued façades of Bellagio

WALK 9
Como Town and Brunate Cable-car

Explore the historic quarter of Como on foot. Visit the glorious Gothic-Renaissance cathedral, hit the shops for fashion and silk – Como was once the centre of Italian silk production – and take a cable-car ride to the village of Brunate for wonderful views across Lake Como.

DISTANCE: 6km (3.5 miles)
TIME: A half day
START/END: Piazza Cavour, Como Town
POINTS TO NOTE: If money is no object, make an advance reservation for dinner in the Villa d'Este (see page 118). Alternatively, a far cheaper option, which also requires advanced booking, is a cruise of the lake with lunch on board or an evening cruise with *aperitivo* (ask at the tourist office at Via Albertolli 7 for details). If escaping the crowds is a priority, download the tourist office's excellent Lake Como is Green guide (in English and Italian) from www.visitcomo.ru.

Como Town

The biggest resort on the lake, **Como Town** is a somewhat disconcerting combination of a historic city and a bustling commercial centre. The town has a fine lakeshore setting, an interesting medieval quarter with cobbled, traffic-free streets and some lustrous shops, but there is nothing approaching the intimacy and timelessness of the small villages beside Lake Como. Whether or not Como conforms to your idea of the perfect holiday resort, it is a handy springboard for exploring the lakes region and has a magnificent setting at the end of the western arm of Lake Como.

Como Town's history

Since its earliest days, when it rose to prominence as a Roman town, Como has been an industrious, aspirational place. Como's most famous sons were Pliny the Elder (AD23–79), the Roman scholar who wrote the 37-volume *Historia Naturalis* (Natural History) and died during the eruption of Vesuvius in AD79, and his nephew and adopted son, Pliny the Younger (AD61–113), an author and lawyer, who is said to have owned at least two villas at Bellagio: one on the hilltop for study and reflection, and another on the lakeshore for hunting and fishing.

In the 11th century, it became a free *comune* (city state), but in 1127 it was destroyed by Milan for having

Piazza Cavour, Como Town

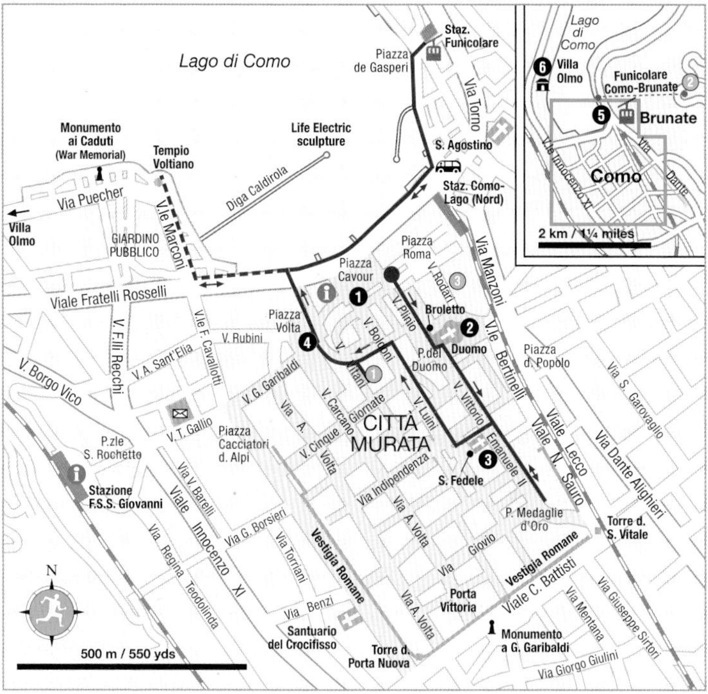

Lago di Como
Staz. Funicolare
Piazza de Gasperi
Via Torno
Monumento ai Caduti (War Memorial)
Tempio Voltiano
Life Electric sculpture
S. Agostino
Diga Caldirola
Staz. Como-Lago (Nord)
Via Puecher
Villa Olmo
GIARDINO PUBBLICO
V.le Marconi
Piazza Roma
Piazza Cavour
V. Rodari
Via Manzoni
Viale Fratelli Rosselli
V. Plinio
Broletto
Piazza Volta
V.le F. Cavallotti
V. Rubini
V. Boldoni
P.del Duomo
Duomo
V.le Bertinelli
Piazza d. Popolo
V. F.lli Recchi
V. A. Sant'Elia
V. Borgo Vico
V. G. Garibaldi
V. Vitani
V. Luini
V. Vittorio Emanuele II
Via S. Garovaglio
V. Carcano
V. Cinque Giornate
CITTÀ MURATA
Viale Lecco
Viale N. Sauro
Via Dante Alighieri
V. T. Gallio
Piazza Cacciatori d. Alpi
Via A. Volta
P.zle S. Rochetto
Via Indipendenza
S. Fedele
Stazione F.S.S. Giovanni
Via V. Bareli
Viale Innocenzo XI
P. Medaglie d'Oro
Torre d. S. Vitale
Via G. Borsieri
Via Torriani
Vestigia Romane
Via Giovio
Via Regina Teodolinda
Via A. Volta
Porta Vittoria
Viale C. Battisti
Via Mentana
Via Giuseppe Sirtori
N
Via Benzi
Santuario del Crocifisso
Torre d. Porta Nuova
Monumento a G. Garibaldi
500 m / 550 yds
Via Giorgo Giulini
Lago di Como
Villa Olmo
Funicolare Como-Brunate
Brunate
V.le Innocenzo XI
Como
Via Dante
2 km / 1¼ miles

sided with Barbarossa, the German Holy Emperor. From 1335 Como came under the sway of the Milanese ruling dynasties, becoming famous for its silk production (see page 12).

The Romanesque style, which is particularly pronounced in Como, has been woven into the city's architectural fabric, from churches to fortified medieval towers. Many monuments also owe much to the craftsmanship of the *maestri comacini*, the medieval master-builders and sculptors of Como, who perfected the Lombard style and became renowned throughout Europe for their remarkable skills.

A town walk

Begin this walk around town at **Piazza Cavour ❶**, the city's waterfront square.

Como's cathedral

Life Electric sculpture by Daniel Libeskind, Lake Como

Como's Duomo

A little way inland along Via Caio Plinio II, **Piazza del Duomo** represents the best introduction to the medieval quarter, centred as it is on the splendidly solemn cathedral. The construction of the **Duomo** ❷ (www.cattedraledicomo.it/en/home-2/; free) began in 1396. Note the impressive gabled façade and observe how it spans the transition in style from late Gothic to Renaissance, with a richly sculpted main portal. Statues of Pliny the Elder and Pliny the Younger occupy the niches to the left and right, respectively.

The interior is slightly gloomy but full of Renaissance works of art, including paintings by Gaudenzio Ferrari (*c.*1471/81–1546) and Bernardino Luini (1480–1532), two Lombard painters who were both influenced by Leonardo da Vinci.

Adjacent to the cathedral is the **Torre del Comune** (bell tower) and the pink-, white- and grey-striped Gothic **Broletto**, the former town hall.

Piazza San Fedele

Take **Via Vittorio Emanuele II**, the main shopping thoroughfare, to Piazza Medaglie d'Oro, then head back towards the waterfront. If you want to take a break for a coffee at this point, check out *Aida*, a historic café and *pasticceria*, at No. 34 on the attractive medieval **Piazza San Fedele** (on the left as you head back along Via Vittorio Emanuele II). Overlooking the square stands the basilica of **San Fedele** ❸ (usually daily 8am–noon, 3.30–7pm, closes earlier in winter), which was thought to be Como's first cathedral. The Lombard-Romanesque church was the work of *Maestri Comacini* (see page 61). It has been much altered over the centuries and was given a new façade in the early 20th century. Note the striking apse at the rear of the church.

Refreshment

From the square, continue towards the lake along **Via Luini**, crossing Via Cinque Giornate for **Bolla** at Via Boldoni 6, one of the best ice cream parlours in Como. Take the first left and left again for **Via Vitani**. At No. 16, the **Osteria del Gallo**, see ①, is ideal for a light lunch.

Piazza Volta

From Via Vitani turn left (east) into Via Muralto and follow the street to **Piazza Volta** ❹. Flanked by boisterous outdoor cafés, the square also has a statue of Count Alessandro Volta (1745–1827), a self-taught physicist who invented the battery and after whom the volt is named. In summer the square is a venue for concerts, as well as occasional sightings of George Clooney, Como's favourite adopted son.

If you wish to investigate Volta's legacy further, then walk to the western side of the harbour where you will find the Neoclassical **Tempio Voltiano** (Volta Temple; Tue–Sun, Apr–Sept 10am–6pm, last admission 5.30pm, closed on

The basilica of San Fedele

Mon; www.visitcomo.eu/en/discover/museums/tempio_voltiano/index.html; charge). On display are Volta's personal effects and the batteries that he invented. Far more exciting is the immense steel Life Electric sculpture rising at the end of the pier. Created by Daniel Libeskind in 2015 of calendared steel, the structure – inspired by sinusoidal waves – includes LED lights and smoke machines for nighttime displays. You can walk out to it along the **Diga Foranea pier** , just below the Tempio.

Sant'Abbondio

In a less salubrious area of Como, southeast of the centre, is the Romanesque gem of **Sant'Abbondio** (Via Sant'Abbondio; daily 8am–6pm, winter 4.30pm; free). The apse is decorated with a remarkable cycle of mid-14th-century frescoes of the life of Christ.

Brunate

Return to Piazza Cavour. If the weather is fine, you might wish to have lunch in **Brunate**, which is set high above the city. Facing the water, turn right and follow the lakeshore north to **Piazza de Gasperi**, passing the city's most upmarket cafés and hotels. The **cable-car** (www.explorelakecomo.com/go/brunate-funicular; charge) ❺ to Brunate leaves every 15 to 30 minutes until midnight in summer (10.30pm rest of the year), and the journey to the summit takes seven minutes. You can also walk up, along the Salita Carescione.

Food and Drink

1 Osteria del Gallo
Via Vitani 16, Como,
www.osteriadelgallo-como.it
Simple, cosy, bistro-like trattoria with home-made dishes. €€

2 Bellavista Hotel & Restaurant
Piazza Bonacossa 2, Brunate,
www.bellavistabrunate.com
Family-run Restaurant Bellavista offers regional dishes based on recipes from the local area. €€

3 Sociale
Via Rodari 6, Como,
www.ristorantesociale.it
Close to the Duomo, the popular Sociale occupies the Palazzo Odescalchi, serving dishes made with local ingredients. €€

Once at the top, you can enjoy your lunch at the **Bellavista Hotel & Restaurant**, see 2, 150m/yds from the cable-car station.

Evening stroll and dinner

In the evening, take a stroll along the waterfront from Piazza Cavour to the **Villa Olmo** ❻ (www.villaolmocomo.it; free). For dining, choose between the **Villa d'Este** in Cernobbio, two ferry stops away, or congenial **Sociale**, see 3, just north of the Duomo.

View over Como from Brunate

TOUR 10
Ramo di Como and Villa del Balbianello

Begin this tour with a romantic cruise along the beautiful Ramo di Como, past waterfront villas and gardens. After a picnic lunch on a haunted island, take a short boat trip to Villa del Balbianello, which has the finest setting on the lake.

DISTANCE: 60km (37-mile), ferry trip (return)
TIME: A full day
START/END: Como Town
POINTS TO NOTE: Check ferry times from any landing stage on the lake or on www.navigazionelaghi.it. Bring a picnic as the once iconic Locanda del Isola Comacina is currently in the centre of a dispute with the local mayor and remains closed at the time of writing in 2023. A useful guide to have with you to find out more about the villas you pass is the tourist offices' bilingual guide to the lake's villas (free download from www.visitcomo.eu/export/sites/default/it/vivere/il-lago-di-como/guidaVille.pdf).

Ramo di Como

From Como, be sure to catch a ferry that stops at Isola Comacina (as some bypass the island). Boats depart from **Piazza Cavour** ❶ on the Como waterfront. The cruise leads to the central part of the lake, famed for its villas and gardens. En route it criss-crosses the most beautiful arm of Lake Como, the **Ramo di Como**, moving from the sunny western side to the shady eastern side. The west has the best resorts, historic villas and gardens; the wilder east is dotted with Romanesque churches and the odd silk factory. This cruise starts at Como, but Isola Comacina and Lenno are also accessible from Bellagio, Tremezzo or any of the ferry stops on the Como–Colico service.

Celebrated villas

On the western shore, **Cernobbio** ❷ is the first major resort after Como. The town has an appealing lakefront and old quarter, but the most eye-catching sights are the 19th-century **Villa Erba**,

Villa d'Este in Cernobbio

which belonged to the family of film director Luchino Visconti before becoming a conference centre, and the **Villa d'Este**, the most prestigious hotel in the lakes (see page 66).

After **Torno** ❸, on the eastern side, you can glimpse in the distance the sombre **Villa Pliniana**, where Byron, Stendhal and Liszt stayed, and where Rossini composed the opera *Tancredi* (1813).

Romantic **Moltrasio** ❹, back on the sunny side of the lake, features the deceptively low-key **Villa Le Fontanelle**, designed as a perfect setting for fashion shows. This was the favourite home of the late Gianni Versace (he had several) – and the one where he lived until he was murdered. The villa was regularly visited by a string of celebrities. After his death it was sold to Russian restaurateur and billionaire Arkady Novikov.

Laglio

The Hollywood star George Clooney bought the Villa Oleandra in the tranquil village of **Laglio** ❺ falling in love with both villa and lake on a motorcycling holiday around the Alps. To thank Clooney for putting Laglio on the map, its mayor has made the actor an honorary citizen of Laglio, and he sits on a committee devoted to preserving the integrity of the lakeside.

Laglio

Yachts and jetties in Laglio

Villa d'Este

The Villa d'Este was built in 1568, when Cernobbio was a village of fishermen and woodcutters. In 1815 Caroline of Brunswick – princess of Wales and future queen of England – fell in love with Lake Como, and persuaded the owner, Countess Pino, to sell her the villa. Caroline spent five years at the Villa d'Este, following a disastrous marriage to the Prince of Wales (the future King George IV). The couple had found each other equally unattractive (he had married 'the vilest wretch this world was ever cursed with' to pay off his debts), and within a year they were living apart. Caroline spent her time embellishing the villa, and leading a lavish and, by all accounts, lascivious lifestyle.

Having run up debts, she returned to London in 1820 in an abortive attempt to take her place on the throne. Legally, Caroline remained Queen Consort until she died at the age of 53. Unlike George IV, she had been popular with the London public, as she had been with the locals of Cernobbio.

Since 1873 the Villa d'Este has been the most luxurious hotel on the lake, hosting royalty, politicians and film stars, and maintaining the elegance of a bygone era. The restaurant offers a less-expensive way to live it up for a while.

Amalfi Coast

The '**Amalfi Coast**' is so named because its dramatic cliffs and wild atmosphere are reminiscent of the real Amalfi Coast near Naples. It begins just to the north of Torno, on the eastern shore.

The fine Romanesque church in **Pognana Lario** sits in the shade of surrounding villas, while **Nesso**, also on the shaded side, is known for a long Romanesque bridge and a gloomy five-storey silk factory that closed in the 1950s, when silk production moved to China, Brazil and Turkey. From Nesso, the ferry crosses to **Argegno** ❻, with its red-tile roofs and sunny lakefront. Perch abound in this, the lake's deepest section.

Isola Comacina

Tiny **Isola Comacina** ❼ is the only island in Lake Como. The very best time to visit is during the **Festival of San Giovanni** (St John), the most magical festival in the lakes, celebrated on 24 June. At other times it is unlike anywhere else on Como, wild, a bit scruffy, with the ruins of nine Romanesque churches.

On the far shore of the lake is the blighted fishing village of **Lezzeno**, in contrast to splendid **Bellagio**, which commands the point beyond. Due to the gigantic shadow cast by the mountains, the sun is permanently

Isola Comacina, the only island on Lake Como

blotted out, and the locals pay the price in terms of tourism.

Haunted island

Tiny though it is, Isola Comacina became a political and military centre in the Middle Ages, acquiring the name of Crispoli, City of Gold. But the island was cursed by the bishop of Como in 1169, probably in revenge for its alliance with Milan, and Como's soldiers razed its churches and forced the inhabitants to take refuge in Varenna. The Baroque **Oratorio di San Giovanni** and the ruins of medieval churches are all that remain. More recently, the island was bequeathed to Belgium's King Albert I, who donated it to the state in 1927. Today it is under the supervision of Milan's Brera Academy of Fine Arts.

Exorcising the demons

In 1949 a passing English journalist by the name of Frances Dale apparently came up with the idea of a 'rite of fire' exorcism to stimulate the tourist trade – and the word spread like wildfire. Today guests at the Locanda are welcomed by the current melancholic master of ceremonies, the bobble-hatted Benvenuto Puricelli (who was born in Sala Comacina, facing the island, and who served a stint as head chef at London's Penthouse Club). Puricelli has been exorcising the island's demons on a daily basis for the past thirty or so years, in which time the roster of visiting international celebrities has included Sylvester Stallone, Michael Schumacher, Madonna, Arnold Schwarzenegger, Brad Pitt and Elton John. The inn's gallery is full of portraits of such stars participating in the theatrical 'purification ceremony'.

The A list

Lake Como is a haven for celebrities, who tend to be discreet and whose privacy is respected. George Clooney has a lovely waterfront villa at Laglio; Sting and Ryanair owner Michael O'Leary have homes on the lake. Guests of the late Gianni Versace at his villa in Moltrasio included Madonna, Elton John and Bruce Springsteen.

Set meal and ceremony

For all the hokum, the set meal – ranging from an array of *antipasti* to chunks of Parmesan, baked onions, grilled trout, chicken and orange ice cream – is good. The rite of fire begins at the flambéed coffee stage, and involves arcane incantations and copious amounts of brandy and sugar. Even if the ceremony is not your cup of capuchin, the lakeside views are

Comacina church

simply gorgeous. After lunch, you may want to follow a path that passes the ruins of the Romanesque churches sacked in 1169.

Good options for lunch are the **Locanda La Tirlindana**, see ①, by the landing stage where boats cross to Isola Comacina, or **Trattoria Santo Stefano**, see ②, on the main square in Lenno.

Villa del Balbianello

Set on the tip of a wooded promontory between Lenno and Sala Comacina, **Villa del Balbianello** ❽ (www.fondoambiente.it; charge) enjoys the loveliest setting on the Italian Lakes. Romance, peace, seclusion, tranquillity and fabulous gardens: this ochre-coloured villa has everything you might hope to find in the region.

To access the villa, you can get a boatman at Isola Comacina to ferry you across, or take the public ferry to nearby Lenno, where you can be taken across in the private shuttle boat (look for the sign at the landing stage). Another option is simply to walk from Lenno to the villa (about 1km/0.6 mile; signposted from the church square).

A cardinal's retreat

In 1786 the sybaritic Cardinal Durini bought the villa here as a retreat from his taxing diplomatic missions. He incorporated what remained of a medieval Franciscan convent, which, with its quaint pair of bell towers, you can still see today. After landscaping this rocky spur, he enlarged the villa, and, as his crowning achievement, added the loggia on the highest point. Durini wanted both a memorable venue for literary salons and a place from which to admire the sun setting in the mountains.

The most recent owner of the villa was the wealthy explorer Count Guido Monzino, a descendant of the cardinal. Acquiring the property in 1954, the count restored the villa and filled it with his collection of books, furniture and works of art. On his death in 1988, he left the villa, complete with contents, to the FAI (the Italian National Trust). Famous for his mountaineering feats and Arctic expeditions – he led a North Pole expedition in 1971 and the first successful Italian ascent of Everest in 1973 – he turned the villa into an international centre for the study of explorations.

Visits of the **villa** take in the library, with hundreds of books devoted to explorations, and a museum full of mountaineering memorabilia, including the sledge on which Monzino trudged to the North Pole in 1971. Fine though the interior is, more

Villa del Balbianello

impressive is the **loggia** when seen from outside: it is covered in climbing plants, and an old fig tree clings to its columns.

The villa has featured in numerous films set in the region. For more on this, see page 137.

Romantic gardens

The **garden** makes the most of its setting on a rocky spur and poor soil conditions. Somewhere between a classical 18th-century Italian affair and a romantic English garden, it exploits the gnarled outline of the barren rock to present beguiling paths that lead up to a three-arched folly. Bound by boxwood and laurel hedges, pergolas, climbing plants and scented wisteria, this secret garden is mirrored in the lake. Cypresses, holm-oaks and plane trees pruned into candelabra shapes provide shelter for snowdrops, cyclamen and magnolia. Closer to the villa are lakeside vistas framed by terracotta tubs of pink hydrangeas and classical statues that protrude from beds of azaleas.

The final view is of the Italian flag unfurled on the jetty, in keeping with Monzino's will. The explorer wanted the gesture to be 'in memory of all the flags my Alpine guides placed on countless peaks all over the world'.

Unless you are up for more adventures, you should ask the boatman to drop you off at the Lenno jetty, where you can take a ferry home.

Food and Drink

1 Locanda La Tirlindana
Piazza Matteotti, Sala Comacina, www.latirlindana.it
Facing Isola Comacina, this charming little *locanda* draws food lovers from all over the world. Frederic extends a warm welcome while Patricia produces mouth-watering ravioli with mascarpone and lemon, sea bass fillet in citrus, and fillet of beef with gorgonzola sauce. On a warm day, you should arrive early (or book in advance) to secure a seat on the terrace, which has glorious views across to the island. It's the perfect spot to enjoy a glass of local wine. €€€

2 Trattoria Santo Stefano
Piazza XI Febbraio 3, Lenno, www.santostefanolenno.it
A small sought-after trattoria where chef Giovanni Sansone produces delicious lake fish-based dishes at affordable prices. Menus change according to the availability of ingredients, but are likely to feature the local 'cucina povera' dish, *missoltino* – small fish that are dried and salted, then fried with vinegar, oil and parsley. €€

The sumptuous view from Villa del Balbianello

Romantic balcony

WALK 11
Bergamo

Bergamo has it all: a majestic setting, a magnificent medieval town, designer shops and gourmet restaurants. This walk takes in one of Italy's richest art museums, then explores the historic Upper Town's piazzas and monuments.

DISTANCE: 4.5km (2.75 miles)
TIME: A full day
START: Accademia Carrera
END: Il Sentierone
POINTS TO NOTE: Avoid driving and parking within Bergamo. There are direct train services from Milan or Como, or, if you are killing time before a flight, buses run every twenty minutes from the nearby Orio al Serio airport (10–15 mins). They stop at the railway station, city centre and funicular station for the Upper Town. Bergamo has a tourist office at Piazzale Guglielmo Marconi, in the Lower Town and another in the Upper Town at Via Gombito 13. The ATB System (www.atb.bergamo.it) is a transportation system for travelling within the city of Bergamo and the 29 surrounding towns by bus, funicular train and the T1 Bergamo-Albino tramway.

Seen from afar, **Bergamo** is a mass of bell towers and domes silhouetted against the Alps. Originally settled by Celts and Romans, the town nevertheless has a Venetian soul, following 400 years of Venetian rule. There are two centres: the historic *Città Alta* (Upper Town) and the more modern *Città Bassa* (Lower Town). The former is bound by a circle of 16th-century walls built by the Venetians after the city expanded beyond its medieval ramparts and fortress.

Lower Town

This walk begins in the Lower Town, laid out in the 1920s with stately tree-lined avenues, porticoes and piazzas.

Accademia Carrara and GAMeC

The **Accademia Carrara** ❶ (Piazza G. Carrara 82; www.lacarrara.it; charge) has a fine collection of Lombard and Venetian art, amassed by a local aristocrat in the 18th century. Among the treasures in this Neoclassical palace are Gothic works by Pisanello and Renaissance and Mannerist works by Bellini, Veronese, Tiepolo, Tintoretto, Raphael and Mantegna. Look out as well for paintings by the very fine local Renaissance artist Lorenzo Lotto.

Funiculars in Bergamo

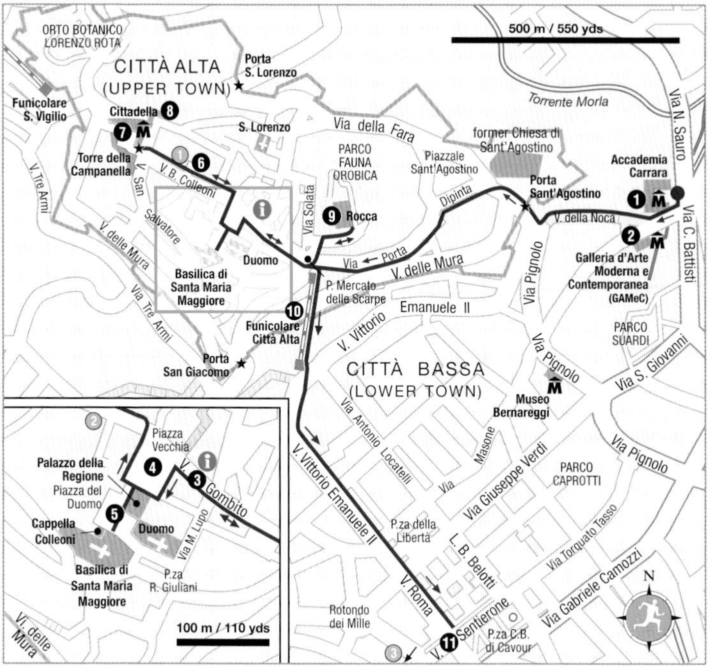

Opposite the Carrara is the **GAMeC** ❷ (Galleria d'Arte Moderna e Contemporanea; Via San Tomaso 53; www.gamec.it; charge), a dynamic gallery housed in a beautifully restored monastery, hosting truly fabulous contemporary art exhibitions – recent exhibitors include Rachel Whiteread and Vivian Suter.

Upper Town

After seeing the Carrara and GAMeC, follow Via della Noca east through the Venetian gateway **Porta Sant'Agostino**, take the Via Porta Dipinta in front of the ex-convent of Sant'Agostino, and climb up into the heart of the **Città Alta**. **Via Gombito** ❸, a lively medieval street lined with food shops and eateries, leads into Piazza Vecchia.

Piazza Vecchia

A showpiece of both medieval and Renaissance monuments surrounding

View down to the Lower Town

Piazza Vecchia in Bergamo city

Donizetti

Bergamo-born composer Gaetano Donizetti (1797–1848) is commemorated in the city by a street, theatre, memorial, monument and museum: the Museo Donizettiano (Via Arena 9; http://museodellestorie.bergamo.it/en/site/museo-donizettiano; Charge) south of the Cittadella.

a fountain with marble lions, the **Piazza Vecchia** ❹ is often described as the most perfect square in Italy.

Flanking the square is the **Palazzo della Ragione** (www.visitbergamo.net/it/dettagli-oggetto/21-palazzo-della-ragione; charge), the much-remodelled medieval council chambers, decorated with a winged Lion of St Mark, the symbol of the Venetian republic. An elegant external stairway leads up to the **main hall**, which houses a collection of fresco panels taken from deconsecrated churches and convents in the region. It also acts as an occasional second venue for Gamec's art exhibitions.

The glass lift of the **Torre Civica** or **Campanone** (www.visitbergamo.net/it/dettagli-oggetto/74-torre-civica---campanone; charge) whisks you up to the top of the tower for fine views. The bell tower chimes 180 times daily at 10pm, in memory of the curfew under the Venetians.

Near the square is Da Franco Ristorante with excellent pizza (see page 118).

Basilica of Santa Maria Maggiore

The religious heart of the town is the adjacent **Piazza del Duomo** ❺, home to both the hybrid **Duomo** with an 1886 façade, and, submerged beneath a sumptuous Baroque interior, the Romanesque basilica of **Santa Maria Maggiore** (www.fondazionemia.it/it/basilica; charge). The church has a beautiful Gothic porch adorned with statues and reliefs and an interior profuse with gilt, stuccowork and paintings.

Colleoni Chapel

Adjoining the church is the ornate **Cappella Colleoni** ❻ (www.visitbergamo.net/it/dettagli-oggetto/18-cappella-colleoni; free), built in 1472–6 as a mausoleum for Bartolomeo Colleoni, a rich Venetian *condottiere* (mercenary), who demolished the sacristy of Santa Maria Maggiore to create the space.

The mausoleum has a marble façade embellished by medallions, columns, sculpture and reliefs. The interior shelters ceiling frescoes by Tiepolo and the tomb of the *condottiere*.

Inspect the railings of the Colleoni Chapel and you will see Colleoni's coat of arms. Called '*i tre colleoni*', the gleaming crest comprises three testicles *(coglioni)* – the third endowed by mother nature.

Museums of Archaeology and Natural History

Return to Piazza Vecchia and head west along **Via B. Colleoni** ❼,

Donizetti's piano

Food and Drink

1 Da Mimmo

Via Colleoni 17; www.damimmoelina.com
Founded in 1956 and still family run, this is a Bergamo institution, serving excellent home-made "Casonsèi de la bergamasca", local ravioli-style pasta with butter, pancetta and sage. The setting is a 14th-century palace and a garden accommodating 200 diners. Reasonably priced set menus. €€

2 Vineria Cozzi

Via Colleoni 22a; www.vineriacozzi.it. An inviting wine bar with a huge choice of Italian wines and a menu of *antipasti*, some fantastic home-made pasta – try casoncelli with hazelnuts and crispy pancetta – vegetarian dishes, including a fabulous grapefruit risotto with crispy veg, cold meats and cheeses. You can also order a two- or three-course picnic, served in a pretty basket with proper tablecloths, something to sit on and cutlery. €€

3 Il Maialino di Giò Piazza

Pontida 37; http://ilmaialinodigio.it
A lively little deli and bar with hams hanging from the ceiling that is particularly popular at *aperitivo* time for its tasty cold cut platters. €

the continuation of Via Gombito. **Da Mimmo**, see 1, and **Vineria Cozzi**, see 2, are good pitstops for lunch or dinner.

At Piazza Mascheroni, pass under the Torre della Campanella for the **Cittadella** 8. A 14th-century fortress used to defend the west section of the city. Today it is home to the **Museo Archeologico** (www.museoarcheologicobergamo.it; charge) and the **Museo di Scienze Naturali** (www.museoscienzebergamo.it; charge).

La Rocca

Retrace your steps back past the cathedral and along Via Gombito to Piazza Mercato delle Scarpe. Divert left from the piazza along Via alla Rocca and climb up to the 14th-century **Rocca** 9, built on the foundations of the Roman capitol, offering impressive views.

Funicular to Lower Town

To return to the lower town, take the 120-year-old **funicular** 10 from Piazza Mercato delle Scarpe. Get off at Viale Vittorio Emanuele II. From here, walk southeast to the tree-lined **Il Sentierone** 11, a favourite rendezvous for the locals and a popular spot for an evening stroll. If you're feeling peckish head to **Il Maialino di Giò Piazza**, see 3, where you can enjoy a glass of wine and some cured meats, reflecting on the highlights of your day.

The Duomo's Baroque ceiling

Colleoni Chapel

TOUR 12
Lake Iseo

Explore the town of Iseo before cruising to the lovely island of Monte Isola for a lakeside stroll and lunch. An afternoon tour of the lake takes in the wild western shore and lakeside villages that retain their medieval core.

DISTANCE: Driving tour: 72km (45 miles)
TIME: A full day
START/END: Iseo
POINTS TO NOTE: Check timetables on www.navigazionelagoiseo.it. The tour of the lake by car is also lovely by ferry.

Unfairly neglected in favour of the larger lakes, **Lake Iseo** (Lago d'Iseo) is more tranquil and less self-consciously quaint. The lake is short on the beautiful attractions that are a hallmark of the other lakes, but compensates with a gentler way of life, fine walks and a delightful unspoilt island to explore.

Iseo

The best base from which to explore the lake is **Iseo** ❶, an attractive historic town that has not completely sold out to tourism. Until the 1870s, it was a significant port that shipped grain from Valle Camonica and steel from the industrial lakeside ports. Today it is a commercial town on a smaller scale. Sandwiched between the waterfront and the feudal Castello Oldofredi, it retains its cosy medieval street pattern and an elegant lakeside promenade.

Historic centre

The liveliest part of town is the porticoed **Piazza Garibaldi**, dominated by a statue of the great patriot perched on a mossy rock – this is one of the few horseless statues of the Risorgimento leader. In Piazza Mazzini, reached by a narrow alley, you can see old stone washtubs and the Arsenale that today serves as an art exhibition venue. Take Via Sombrico and Via delle Pieve for the church of **Sant'Andrea**. Although clumsily remodelled, it has the finest Romanesque bell tower in the region. To the southwest, the restored 15th-century **Castello Oldofredi** is set on a mound and is home to the little **Museo delle due Guerre** (closed for refurbishment at the time of writing, for updates see http://visitlakeiseo.info/

View of Monte Isola from the water

en/arts-and-culure/the-two-wars-museum), where two rooms house equipment used in World Wars I and II, including military uniforms, firearms and hand grenades.

Monte Isola

Return to Piazza Garibaldi and make for the lakeside, where you can take a relaxing ferry ride to **Peschiera Maraglio** ❷ on **Monte Isola**, usually the second stop. The mountainous, densely forested island – the largest lake island in Europe – supports a 200-strong community of fishermen, boatbuilders and net-makers.

Car-free island

The pace of life is palpably slow here: private cars are banned (though local motorbikes are not) and a minibus service connects the various hamlets. The fishing hamlets reveal refined touches, from sculpted portals to tiny courtyards and loggias. Above, tiers of olive groves merge into vineyards and chestnut groves. The highest peak is surmounted by the 16th-century **Santuario Madonna della Ceriola**, built over a pagan shrine.

Lunch at Peschiera Maraglio

Choose a typical lakeside haunt at Peschiera Maraglio (which is also known simply as 'Peschiera') for an outdoor lunch. After you have had your fill of grilled sardines, perch risotto and lake scampi, check out the cluttered shop on the waterfront that sells fishing nets and hammocks: net-making is an integral part of life on the island. An industry thought to have been initiated by Cluniac monks 1,000 years ago now embraces Wimbledon

tennis nets and World Cup football nets. Depending on the season and time of day, there may be signs of boatbuilders at work or fishermen laying their catch out to dry in the sun.

Peschiera to Sensole

The best gentle walk from Peschiera west is along the lakeside path to **Sensole** ❸, taking in views of competent swimmers competing for attention with struggling ducks. Both hamlets are set on the sunny side of Monte Isola, and the view encompasses the tiny island of San Paolo with the town of Iseo melting into the background. If you have not already eaten, you might consider **La Spiaggetta**, see ①, between the villages. The alternative to walking is to hire a bike at Peschiera – you can cycle round the whole island in about fifty minutes.

Western shore

Catch the ferry back to Iseo, then take a scenic drive clockwise around the lake (following signs west to Sarnico) to see Riva di Solto's rugged western shore in Bergamo province.

Clusane

Just to the west of Iseo, **Clusane** ❹ is a food-lover's paradise: on the waterfront there are fine fish restaurants that specialise in baked tench. Crowned by a castle, Clusane overlooks a busy port full of traditional red- and yellow-rimmed fishing boats setting out in search of tench, pike, chub and lake sardines. The village borders wine-growing Franciacorta, and its hinterland is dotted with inns. You may wish to return to Clusane for dinner.

Sarnico to Riva di Solto

The first resort on the western shore (5km/3 miles), **Sarnico** occupies the site of a prehistoric stilt village and owes much of its character to the ruined medieval ramparts and graceful loggias. But it is best known for its speedboat companies that support one of the lake's premier activities.

Follow the lakeshore road for 20.5km (12.75 miles) to Riva di Solto. From over-quarried Tavernola Bergamasca to Riva di Solto lies the most dramatic stretch of the western shore, with coves carved into limestone cliffs and sheer ravines running down to gnarled rocks. These jagged formations reputedly inspired Leonardo da Vinci's *Virgin of the Rocks* and possibly the *Mona Lisa*.

Riva di Solto ❺ is a pretty fishing hamlet full of alleys and arches, with placid views across to the domesticated shore of Monte Isola.

Lovere

After 7km (4.5 miles) is **Lovere** ❻, dominating the northern end of the lake. Originally a Venetian textile town, Lovere turned to steel then

Marone town on Lake Iseo

watersports tourism. Stroll along the waterfront with its lakeside cafés and restaurants, and then explore the historic core with its narrow alleys, medieval towers, castle remains and the frescoed Renaissance church of **Santa Maria in Valvendra**.

On the lakefront, the Neoclassical Palazzo Tadini is home to the Galleria dell'Accademia Tadini (www.accademia tadini.it; charge), displaying works of the Lombard and Venetian schools, including Tintoretto, Jacopo Bellini and Giandomenico Tiepolo.

Eastern shore

The eastern shore is less peaceful, and between Pisogne and Marone you will be driving through tunnels. Pisogne can be clearly seen across the water from Lovere but has to be accessed by taking the main Via Nazionale (SS42) north, beyond the northern tip of the lake, and then heading south along the SP55, signposted to Pisogne.

Pisogne

The former arms-manufacturing town of **Pisogne** ❼ was a centre of commerce for the whole valley in medieval times, and retains an appealing historic centre. The main square is the spacious **Piazza del Mercato**, overlooking the lake and flanked by arcades. Looking onto the square is the medieval **Torre del Vescovo** (Bishop's Tower), where (according to one of the rather

The Camonica Valley

North of Lake Iseo, the Camonica Valley (Valle Camonica, www.turismovalle camonica.it; free) has been inhabited since the Neolithic era. As long ago as 8,000 BC, hunters were recording scenes of everyday life by carving on the smooth sandstone rocks of the valley floor. Some 180,000 etchings have been discovered, constituting the greatest concentration of prehistoric rock carvings in Europe. These are scattered all along the valley, but the best examples are contained within Capo di Ponte's **Parco Nazionale delle Incisioni Rupestri** (National Park of Rock Engravings; www.parcoincisioni. capodiponte.beniculturali.it; free), a Unesco World Heritage Site.

Although the Camonica Valley is nowadays partially marred by industry, the park is rural and wild, with birch and pine woods. The primitive carvings span several thousand years, from Stone Age scratchings to Bronze Age narratives to Roman graffiti. Animals – from Etruscan boxer dogs masked as cockerels to elk speared by hunters and deer caught in lassoes – feature prominently. However, unless you are an expert or have booked a guide (www.guideturisticheilmosaico. com), the mysteries can be hard to decipher, and the routes are not as clearly marked as you might expect from a World Heritage Site.

Lake fish hanging out to dry

Food and Drink

1 La Spiaggetta
Via Sensole 26, Monte Isola, www.facebook.com/LaSpiaggettawakeclub
This little family-run trattoria serves coffees, light food – including excellent sandwiches – and drinks on the lakeside path between Sensole and Pescheria Maraglio. €

finely illustrated information panels in the town centre) those who defaulted on taxes were hung in a cage fixed to the tower, and where, in 1518, eight women accused of witchcraft were imprisoned before being burned alive in the square.

Chiesa di Santa Maria della Neve

On the outskirts of the town (follow signs for 'Affreschi del Romanino'), the church of **Santa Maria della Neve** (www.visitlakeiseo.info/en/arts-and-culure/church-of-santa-maria-della-neve; free) is known as 'La Cappella Sistina dei Poveri' (the Poor Man's Sistine Chapel) on account of the striking frescoes covering the walls and ceiling. Depicting scenes from *The Passion of Christ*, the works are by Romanino (c.1484–1559), a leading Brescian Renaissance artist known for his realistic portraits – which can be found all around Lake Iseo.

Zone Nature Reserve

Continuing 10km (6.25 miles) south along the lake you come to **Marone**, overlooking the diminutive, privately owned **Isola di Loreto** (Loreto Island), where trees cluster around a castle.

A twisting road inland from here takes you to **Zone** (7km/4.25 miles), a picturesque village renowned for the **Riserva Naturale Piramidi di Zone** **8**. This unique formation of 'erosion pillars', created by uneven glacial erosion, is the finest example in Europe. Their most unusual features are the boulders that are precariously perched on top, looking like hats. The best views of these 'stone fairies' (as the locals call them) is at **Cislano**, before you get to Zone.

Dinner options

Return to Marone and follow the road south for Iseo (13km/8 miles) to complete the circuit.

For dinner, shoot past Sulzano, unless you intend to take the ferry back to Monte Isola for another fish feast (the ferry only takes fifteen minutes from here). Clusane is a better bet than Iseo for dining out. A good option is **Punta dell'Est** (see page 118). Alternatively, walk or drive inland from Clusane 1.5km (1 mile) for the enchanting **Relais Mirabella** (see page 119), signposted from the main road.

Another lovely setting with first-class food is the **Relais I Due Roccoli** (see page 119), at Polaveno, 12km (7.5 miles) east of Iseo.

Fresco of 'The Last Supper' in the church of Santa Maria della Neve in Pisogne

TOUR 13
The Franciacorta wine trail

This leisurely drive in the prestigious wine-growing region of Franciacorta takes you through rolling vine-clad hills, past castles, villas and wineries. The trip starts with a visit to a Cluniac monastery and ends with dinner in Clusane.

DISTANCE: 60km (37 miles)
TIME: A half day
STAR ISEO
END: Clusane
POINTS TO NOTE: The majority of the wine estates require prior notice for visits and are only open on specific weekends. The Associazione Strada del Vino Franciacorta, the local wine-growers' association (www.franciacorta.wine/en) can arrange visits to wineries for individuals or as part of a tour. There are also recommended routes for cyclists and walkers, ranging from two to three hours to a couple of days.

The scenic Franciacorta region south of Iseo is renowned mainly for sparkling wines, but also dry, velvety whites and medium-bodied reds. The rolling countryside is dotted with manor houses and villas, many of which have been transformed into wine estates or inns.

Free Court

In the 11th century, local nobles called on Cluniac monks to drain the land around Franciacorta. The results were beneficial to both parties: the local economy received a boost, and the way was paved, literally, for the building of impressive new monasteries. The ecclesiastical authorities appreciated the local climate and countryside to the extent that the village of Borgonato became the summer residence of monks from Brescia's Santa Giulia monastery. The secular authorities granted tax concessions, which led to the region's nickname of Corte Franca (Free Court). This in turn encouraged patrician families from Brescia and beyond to build villas in the mellow hills here. Wealthy restaurateurs and viticulturists followed in their wake, and Franciacorta was on the way to becoming the sought-after retreat it is today.

Nature reserve

Coming out of Iseo take a right turn on to the old road to Brescia

Tasty white wine

(avoiding the newer SP510). You will soon see the **Riserva Naturale Torbiere del Sebino ❶** on your right. This former peat bog is the watery domain of tench, trout and eel. It is also home to a variety of predatory birds, from herons to kingfishers. You can stroll along the paths that go through the peat bogs.

San Pietro in Lamosa

Towards the southern end of the reserve is the little Cluniac monastery of **San Pietro in Lamosa ❷** (www.visitlakeiseo.info; charge). It sits on a small rise on the right above the road (it is roughly 5km/3 miles from Iseo and easy to miss, so go slowly). Comprising four chapels, the monastery was founded in the 11th century and added to over the centuries. Volunteer restorers have revealed a number of frescoes – some dating back to Gothic times.

Franciacorta wine trail

Monticelli Brusati

Head south to Camignone, then follow the marked Franciacorta wine route (marked Strada del Vino Franciacorta) east to **Monticelli Brusati ❸** and vineyards that stretch out as far as the eye can see. The village is home to **La Montina** winery (Via Baiana 17; http://lamontina.com) set around the beautiful Villa Baiana. Monticelli Brusati is also the splendid setting for the **Azienda Agricola Villa** wine estate (follow signs for Villa), complete with farm-stay homes and a simple Osteria-style restaurant (www.villa franciacorta.it) that serves pasta, fresh *antipasti* and superb wines.

Many wine estates open for tours and tastings during the Festival of Franciacorta in mid-September.

Bornato

Retrace your route to Camignone, then drive southwest to **Passirano**,

Monastery of San Pietro in Lamosa

home to a striking medieval castle. Follow signs for the next village, **Bornato**, where the **Castello di Bornato** ❹ (Via Castello 24; www.castellodibornato.com; charge) has wonderful views of Franciacorta. A crenellated medieval castle, it opens onto a Renaissance villa and Italianate gardens. This is a small wine estate, with tasting included in the visit.

Erbusco

If lunch is now a consideration, you could stop at the **Trattoria del Gallo**, see ①, at **Rovato**, or head on to **Erbusco** ❺, the unassuming stone-built village at the centre of the wine district. Here you can dine and drink as the locals do at **Cadebasi**, see ②.

Corte Franca

After Erbusco, still following the wine route signs, you reach **Corte Franca**, the heart of the wine region, consisting of four villages: Borgonato, Timoline, Colombaro and Nigoline.

Dinner in Clusane

A return to the lakeshore at **Sarnico** marks the end of the tour. When heading to Iseo, you could stop at the charming fishing village of **Clusane** ❻, known for its traditional baked-tench cuisine. **Trattoria Al Porto**, see ③, in the centre, just back from the lake, is recommended.

Food and Drink

① Trattoria del Gallo

Via Cantine 10, Rovato, www.trattoriadelgallo.it

This retro-looking trattoria serves simple local cuisine with some interesting twists – such as carrot gnocchi with rabbit and Jerusalem artichoke. Typical dishes are steak, rabbit or donkey, pastas with *funghi* or truffles, or meat-filled ravioli in a buttery sage sauce. They also do cooking classes followed by dinner. €€

② Cadebasi

Via Cavour 11, Erbusco; 030-836 7340

Popular with locals and travellers alike. Their extensive wine and drink menu pairs perfectly with finger foods and entrees. €€

③ Trattoria Al Porto

Porto dei Pescatori, Clusane www.alportoclusane.it

This inviting trattoria by Lake Iseo has been run by the same family since 1862. It is renowned for *tinca al forno* (baked tench) with polenta, as well as other freshwater fish. The restaurant's rustic interior, adorned with vintage fishing gear and historical photos, adds to its authentic charm. €€

Franciacorta vineyards in the Brescia province

Restored fresco in San Pietro

WALK 14
Sirmione

Explore Sirmione, steeped in history and enticingly set on a finger-like peninsula pointing into the southern end of Lake Garda. This walk takes you from the fairy-tale Scaligeri castle to the evocative ruins of the Grottoes of Catullus, one of the finest Roman patrician residences in northern Italy.

DISTANCE: 3.5km (2 miles)
TIME: A half day
START/END: Rocca Scaligera
POINTS TO NOTE: Sirmione's Old Town is closed to traffic except for residents and hotel guests, so park as near as you can to the entrance by the drawbridge. In season and on Fridays (market day) and Sundays this could be in a car park 10–15 mins walk away. A little electric train links the centre with the Grotte di Catullo, though it's not far to walk. Be prepared for narrow alleys packed with tourists, especially from May to September. Pick up a map and other information from the tourist office (www.visitsirmione.com) near the entrance of the historic centre at Viale Marconi.

The Romans were drawn to the invigorating waters around Lake Garda and, impressed by Sirmione's hot, sulphurous springs, developed the spa as a sybaritic retreat. The conquering Scaligeri counts from Verona recognised Sirmione's military potential and built a medieval fortress from which to govern the southern part of the lake. From the 15th until the end of the 18th century the town was subject to Venetian rule. In spite of recent over-commercialisation, it retains much of its architectural grace.

Rocca Scaligera

To enter the historic quarter, cross the drawbridge over the duck and fish-filled moat for the 13th-century **Rocca Scaligera** ❶ (Piazza Castello; www.museilombardia.cultura.gov.it; charge). Crowned by swallow-tailed battlements and encircled by water, the fort has guarded the entrance to the historic centre for eight centuries. It was built by the Veronese Scaligeri dynasty, who ruled Verona from 1260–1387. In addition to the moat, the castle features well-preserved bastions and crenellations and a fortified dock. The main attraction is wandering around the battlements and climbing

Aerial view of Sirmione

up the towers for views. A recognisable feature of the tyrannical Scaligeri dynasty are castles with fishtail battlements. Sirmione's Rocca Scaligera is a fine example, but there are several others dotted around Lake Garda.

Opposite the castle, you will find the tiny 14- to 15th-century church of **Santa Anna della Rocca**. It was also constructed by the Scaligeri family, and for centuries served as a place of pilgrimage.

Via Vittorio Emanuele

From the castle, follow the flow along Via Vittorio Emanuele, the main street leading northwards, and take the first right by the Bar Scaligeri, then under the arch and right again for the pretty 15th-century church of **Santa Maria Maggiore** ❷ (free), which overlooks a pebble beach. The church has a pretty portico which incorporates a Roman capital. The lakeside promenade by the beach provides a peaceful route to the Grottoes of Catullus for those who prefer to steer clear of the crowded centre. Follow the beach to the Lido delle Bionde (www.lidodellebionde.it/; charge), where you can swim in the lake, take out a pedalo or have a snack at the café. The Grottoes of Catullus are signposted from the lido. When the lake water is low, you can walk right around the peninsula below the grottoes.)

On the same street as the church you will find **La Fiasca**, see ①. The surrounding web of tiny alleys abounds in gelaterias, overpriced art galleries, souvenirs and outlets selling chic handcrafted jewellery.

Spa centre

Via Vittorio Emanuele continues northwards to the modern spa centre of **Terme di Sirmione** (www.termedisirmione.com;

Crossing the drawbridge of the Rocca Scaligera

Piazza Carducci

Sirmione's spas

In 1889 a Venetian diver called Procopio inserted a long pipe into the lake rocks near the Grottoes of Catullus and released a jet of hot sulphurous water. The discovery led to the delicate operation of laying 300m (984ft) of pipes to bring up the steaming waters from the bottom of the lake. Sirmione's first spa centre opened in 1900, and today around 650,000 guests arrive annually for treatment. The waters are rich in sodium chloride, bromine and iodine, and are used for treating respiratory and rheumatic diseases, as well as for beauty and well-being programmes. The Terme combines spa centres and four hotels with thermal facilities. The Aquaria wellness centre offers access for two or five hours plus a variety of day pass programmes (up to six days), where you can make the most of thermal pools, bubbling beds, hydro-massage, and aromo-chromatic showers. Alternatively, if you want to spare the expense and time, just pop into a pharmacy and purchase a bottle of Acqua di Sirmione or Sirmiogel – both composed of 100 per cent Sirmione spa water.

charge) on Piazza Piatti. Here the hot sulphur springs – bubbling waters are channelled up from the bottom of the lake – are utilised in the treatment of an assortment of respiratory complaints.

Church of San Pietro

From Piazza Piatti take Via Punta Staffalo, which leads to the western shore. Turn right along Via San Pietro, a turning to the north, which brings you to the church of **San Pietro** ❸. This Romanesque church, the oldest in Sirmione, was constructed on top of the remains of a Roman temple and remodelled with recycled Roman bricks.

A lane links the church to the Via Caio Valerio Catullo, leading north to the Grottoes of Catullus.

Grottoes of Catullus

Around the end of the promontory, medieval Sirmione can be explored to its Roman core. Crowning the rocky top of the peninsula, and once reached via a triumphal arch and barrel-vaulted arcades, the **Grotte di Catullo** ❹ (Via Catullo; www.museilombardia.cultura.gov.it; charge) are the remains of a vast Roman villa and spa complex, constituting one of the most important examples of a Roman patrician residence in northern Italy.

The site was named after Rome's greatest lyric poet, who was said to have languished here when rejected by Lesbia, his mistress in Rome. However, although the pleasure-seeking poet makes reference to a home in

Remains of the Grottoes of Catullus

Sirmione close to his heart, the general consensus of opinion is that this villa dates from a slightly later period.

The ruins

Marking the entrance to the ruins is a museum (wintertime open 8.30am–7.30pm, rest of the year hours are as Grottoes of Catullus), which displays some beautiful fresco fragments and mosaics discovered at the villa, along with grave finds and sculptural fragments from other parts of Sirmione.

The ruins cover some 2ha (5 acres) of the promontory and are set high above the lake amid olive and cypress trees. A geometric puzzle, the ruins reveal a complex interplay of passages and porticoes – a sensitive blending of brick and rough-hewn stone. The most imposing remains are on the north side, with rooms up to 12m (39ft) long. Deciphering the rooms on the various levels is not easy, but there are plaques on the site showing how the villa was constructed, what the rooms were for and how it would have looked in all its glory. In any event, it is lovely just to wander around the ruins and admire the views.

Eating options

For restaurants, head back towards the castle. If your feet are weary at the end of the day, take the little **Trenino Elettrico** (electric train), which provides a shuttle service (for a small charge) between the Grottoes of Catullus and the Terme Catullo at Piazza Piatti.

Sirmione is packed with take-away pizza places but for proper food in a pretty setting try **Osteria Al Torcol**, see 2 or splash out on gourmet fare at **La Rucola** (see page 121), close to the castle. If you are taking a ferry home, you might be tempted to wait for your boat at the **Risorgimento** (see page 121), on Piazza Carducci where the ferries depart.

Food and Drink

1 La Fiasca

Via Santa Maria Maggiore 11; www.trattorialafiasca.it

This central trattoria is a cut above the average tourist Sirmione fare. No-frills classics, regional dishes and home-made pastas and fresh fish are served. €€

2 Osteria Al Torcol

Via San Salvatore 30; 030-990 4605

Authentic home-cooked fare at reasonable prices makes this a rare find for tourist-packed Sirmione. It is small, family-run and highly popular. Book in advance if you can, ideally for the vine-clad garden on a warm evening. €€

The view from the ruins

Unwind at Terme Catullo

TOUR 15
Lake Garda cruise

Lake Garda's scenery is enormously diverse, from the sea-like southern basin, fringed by beaches, to the fjord-like north, where the Brenta Dolomites drop sheer into the water. This full-day cruise takes in Riviera-like shores, lakeside villages and historic castles and harbours.

DISTANCE: Hydrofoil from Sirmione to Malcesine: 60km (37 miles); return trip: 120km (75 miles)
TIME: A full day
START/END: Sirmione
POINTS TO NOTE: Make an early start and take one of the fast routes (marked in red on the timetable – www.navigazionelaghi.com) to get to Malcesine for lunch. The boat will make several stops en route, but you will only have time to disembark at one destination other than Malcesine. Recommended are either Gargnano or Bardolino. If you are limited to half a day, concentrate on the lower lake only. This trip starts at Sirmione, but you can also go from other resorts on the southern shore, such as Desenzano del Garda or Peschiera del Garda.

Cruising the lake is far more relaxing than coping with traffic-filled lakeshore roads and dimly lit tunnels. It is also the best way to admire the scenery.

Approximately 51km (32 miles) long and 17km (10.5. miles) wide at its maximum point, Garda is Italy's largest lake. Apart from some spectacular scenery, it offers fine beaches and clean, warm waters. The area enjoys a wide range of climatic conditions, from chilly Alpine glaciers north of the lake to Mediterranean warmth.

In the Middle Ages, ruling dynasties built splendid defences around the lake's shores; in the 19th century European aristocrats and literati came for the healthy climate. Although picturesque villages still dot the shorelines and medieval castles rise from the waters, it is nowadays the most crowded of the Italian lakes, with large numbers of German and Austrian holidaymakers, sailors and windsurfers descending on its shores. The south in particular has seen major commercialisation.

Bardolino

From the ferry landing stage off Piazza Carducci in **Sirmione ❶**,

Touring the lake by boat

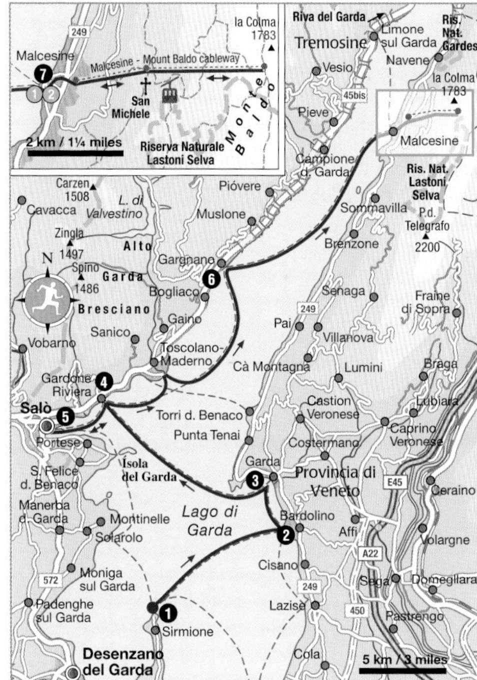

take the fast service to **Bardolino** ❷ on the Veneto shore, framed by rolling hills and vine-clad slopes. Bardolino Superiore now has DOCG status; to learn more about the delicious cherryish-red wine, visit the excellent **Museo del Vino** (Wine Museum; Via Costabella 9, Bardolino; www.museodelvino.it; free). In the adjoining Zeno winery, you can taste whites and rosés as well as the reds, and purchase bottles from two or three euros.

A half hour walk will take you to the **Museo dell'Olio di Oliva** (Olive Oil Museum; Via Peschiera 54, Cisano di Bardolino; www.museum.it; free), with a shop selling olives, honey and pasta, as well as olive oil. Wine and food aside, the town has a ruined castle, two Romanesque churches and a medieval quarter.

Garda

The lake took its name from the town of **Garda** ❸, which shelters in the lee of a huge rocky outcrop. Lake Garda was once called Benacus (Beneficient) – and it is occasionally still referred to by the Latin name. The former fishing village is now a popular resort, with a long café-lined promenade that you can see from the boat, and narrow alleys packed with *trattorie* and souvenirs.

The Limoni Riviera

From Garda the boat crosses the lake to **Gardone Riviera** ❹ and

Shaft of sunlight over the waters of Garda

Limone sul Garda

Several boats, including a car ferry and private excursion boats, link Malcesine with the busy resort of Limone on the Lombardy shore. Less self-consciously cute than Sirmione, Limone is caught between lush Mediterranean vegetation and sheer rock faces that cower under snow-clad peaks. D.H. Lawrence adored Limone, which, he wrote, overlooked 'a lake as beautiful as the beginning of creation'. What was once an old fishing port is today very touristy. You might assume the village is named after the citrus fruit, but it is more likely that the name derives from the Latin *limen* (border), referring to the former frontier here between Austria and Italy.

Salò ❺, two prestigious resorts on the Lombardy bank, whose elegant promenades you can admire from the boat. (If you have time another day, they are covered in detail on tour 16; see page 90).

Lemon terraces

The boat now skirts the loveliest stretch of coast, where wild Alpine terrain stretches all the way to **Riva del Garda**. Despite the cliffs, the area is a hothouse for Mediterranean shrubs and citrus fruits as a result of the balmy microclimate.

Citrus fruits, introduced by medieval monks, used to constitute the lake's cash crop. To protect the lemons from rare but catastrophic cold spells, the terraces were traditionally south-facing, covered with wooden supports in the colder months, and watched over by gardeners who would light fires if the temperature dropped suddenly. Citrus cultivation went into an irreversible decline in the 19th century, with competition from cheaper citrus fruits grown in the hotter climate of southern Italy. These distinctive but mostly defunct *limonaie* (lemon terraces), with their rows of white stone pillars, still dot the lakeshore from Gargnano, north of Gardone, to **Limone sul Garda**. The Limonaia del Castel in Limone (www.visitlimonesulgarda.com; Nominal charge) and the Limonaia Prà de la Fam in Tignale (www.ecomuseopradelafam.com; Nominal charge) are two of the few that have been preserved and can be seen in operation.

Gargnano

From Gardone it is a short hop to **Maderno**, twinned with neighbouring **Toscolano**, and used mainly by tourists for its car ferry service across to **Torri del Benaco** on the opposite side of the lake. Going north, **Gargnano** ❻ is one of the main sailing centres on the lake. Remarkably unspoilt, it has a lively little port, a promenade

Gargnano sailing centre

of orange trees, some charming hotels and several gourmet restaurants. With time in hand, alight here and take a leisurely stroll before boarding the next boat to Malcesine.

Malcesine

Alight at family-friendly **Malcesine** 7, the loveliest resort on the Veneto shore, with a café-lined waterfront, balconied Venetian-style houses and a maze of cobbled alleys. Choose from one of the many restaurants, ranging from simple *osterie*, such as **Osteria Santo Cielo**, see 1, to gourmet haunts such as **Trattoria Vecchia Malcesine**, see 2, and **Ristorante Re Lear** – surely the only restaurant in the world to be named after King Lear. (see page 121).

Scaligero Castle

The village clusters below the crenellated **Castello Scaligero** (www.visitmalcesine.com/en/the-scaliger-castle-of-malcesine; charge), whose battlements and tower command fine views of the lake. Within the walls is a **natural history museum**.

Monte Baldo Cable-Car

Behind the resort you will find Malcesine's state-of-the-art **funicular** (www.funiviedelbaldo.it; charge), which links the resort to the summit of **Monte Baldo** (2,218m/7,275ft). The panoramic rotating cable-cars whisk you up there in a matter of minutes, stopping en route at San Michele. The mountain ridge offers spectacular views, scenic walking trails and a profusion of flora. In winter the cable-car goes up to the ski slopes.

Cruise back to Sirmione, alighting, if you haven't already, at Bardolino en route.

In late September and early October Bardolino hosts the Festa dell'Uva (Grape Festival) where corks pop nonstop.

Food and Drink

1 Osteria Santo Cielo

Piazza Turazza 11, Malcesine; 348-745 1345

An excellent spot for a light lunch, with salads, salamis, tapas and cheese, plus a good choice of wine. The setting is simple and rustic, with a cellar-like interior and tables outside. €

2 Trattoria Vecchia Malcesine

Via Pisort 6, Malcesine, www.vecchiamalcesine.com

A tiny gourmet trattoria tucked away on a scenic terrace in the old quarter with wonderful views of the castle and lake. The Michelin-starred cuisine includes local delicacies such as duck confit with Parmesan and truffles, ravioli with snails, and prawns with garlic butter. Book in advance. €€€€

Drinks at Limone sul Garda

Rock faces beside the town

TOUR 16
Gardone Riviera

On the western shore of Lake Garda, Gardone Riviera maintains much of the elegance that drew the rich, royal and famous in the late 19th century. A visit to botanical gardens and Il Vittoriale degli Italiani, the most eccentric residence on the lakes, is followed by a ferry trip to the historic resort of Salò.

DISTANCE: Gardone Riviera to Salò by ferry: 4km (2.5 miles)
TIME: A half day
START: Gardone Riviera
END: Salò
POINTS TO NOTE: If you are not driving, there are regular ferries to Gardone Riviera from Sirmione, Desenzano del Garda or Peschiera del Garda. If a trip to Isola del Garda appeals, check out the times of boats from Salò and book a guided tour in advance. If the tour is in the morning, start at Salò and visit Gardone Riviera in the afternoon as it is a nice place to wind down with an evening drink.

It was the mild climate that attracted the Austrian emperor and other members of the European elite to build palatial villas here in the 1880s, as **Gardone Riviera** became the most fashionable resort on the lake. It retains luxury hotels, some fine villas, a promenade lined with oleanders, palms and orange trees, and a beach for lake swimming. The guest list at the *belle époque* **Grand Hotel** ❶, which stands prominently on the waterfront, includes Somerset Maugham, Vladimir Nabokov and Winston Churchill.

Giardino André Heller

Just off the lakeside promenade, the **Giardino André Heller** ❷ (www.hellergarden.com; charge) is an oasis of flora created in 1912 by Arturo Hruska, a passionate botanist and dentist to the last czar of Russia. It is a peaceful spot with pretty rockeries, English and Japanese gardens, and an Alpine garden with ravines chiselled out of the rocks.

Il Vittoriale

Take a left turn after the botanical gardens and climb up to **Gardone Sopra**, the oldest part of town. This is the site of a much-visited, somewhat bizarre villa, secluded by cypresses and oleanders. **Il Vittoriale degli**

Villa in Gardone Riviera

Italiani ❸ (www.vittoriale.it; charge) is a testament to the megalomania of Gabriele D'Annunzio (1863–1938). A soldier, poet, Fascist, aviator, aesthete and womaniser, he occupies an odd place in Italian hearts, somewhere between reverence and bafflement. 'Destiny calls me towards Lake Garda,' he declared, although it was actually Mussolini who presented him with the villa in 1925.

The dictator and the poet

Disillusioned with the paltry gains won by Italy in the post-World War I peace – the Dalmatian town of Fiume (Rijeka; now part of Croatia) on the Adriatic had been promised to Italy but was presented to Yugoslavia instead – D'Annunzio and his private army occupied Fiume. Forced to withdraw in 1921, D'Annunzio retired to Lake Garda.

Decadent decor

Named in celebration of Italy's victory over Austria in 1918, and remodelled by D'Annunzio, the 18th-century Il Vittoriale is one of Italy's most flamboyant pre-war estates. The house, known as the **Prioria**, has two reception rooms, one cold and formal for disliked guests (including Mussolini), the other a warmer chamber where his favourites were welcomed. D'Annunzio's delusions of grandeur led him to create a low entrance to his study, so guests had to stoop, presumably to bow. D'Annunzio abhorred daylight, so the windows were made of stained glass or painted over. When the penumbra became too much to bear, D'Annunzio would retreat to the coffin in the Sala di Lebbroso.

The **Museo della Guerra** (War Museum) documents D'Annunzio's military enterprises, displaying uniforms, medals for bravery, banners and numerous photographs.

Isola del Garda

Off the headland south of Salò is the Isola del Garda (Garda Island). For centuries this was a monastery island, and the first religious community was said to have been founded on the island by St Francis of Assisi. Since the dissolution of the monastery by Napoleon, the island has been in private hands. The present owners are the Cavazza family. When Count Cavazza died, he left the island to Lady Charlotte Chetwynd Talbot and her seven children. It is open to two-hour-long guided tours (advance bookings via website required; www.isoladelgarda.com; charge). Boats leave from several harbours in the lower lake, including Salò.

Relics of the Fiume Fiasco

The splendour of the grounds contrasts with the ugliness of the creations that inhabit them: a magnolia grove houses

Mausoleum of Gabriele D'Annunzio

Hruska Botanical Garden

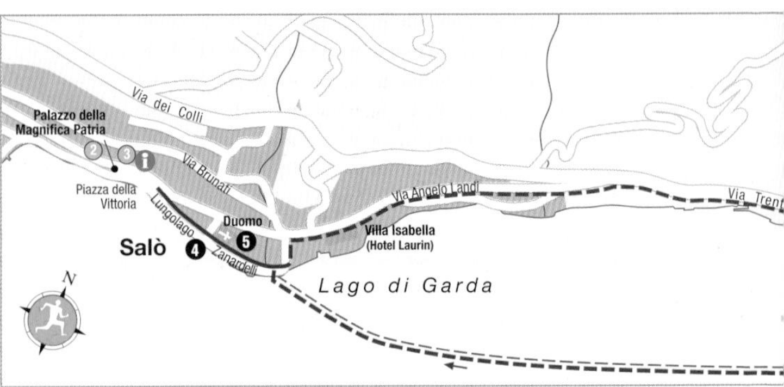

Food and Drink

1 Agli Angeli
Via Dosso 7, Gardone Riviera,
www.agliangelilocanda.it
Trattoria near Il Vittoriale, with a lovely terrace for summer dining. Typical dishes are hand-made pasta, locally-sourced meat, and lake fish and the menu changes month to month. €€€

2 Osteria dell'Orologio
Via Butturini 26, Salò,
www.osteriadellorologiosalo.eatbu.com
There's a Slow Food emphasis here with traditional dishes based on locally-sourced ingredients – such as seasonal soups, pasta with local Bagoss cheese, slow-cooked suckling pork, and fish sourced from the lake. Excellent wine list. €€

3 Osteria di Mezzo
Via di Mezzo 10, Salò;
www.osteriadimezzo.it
One of Salò's best restaurants, set in vaulted cellars in the centre. Traditional dishes with a contemporary twist, with all ingredients rigorously sourced from small-scale local producers. They make their own bread, pasta and desserts. €€€

a war memorial, while the *Puglia* ship that featured in the Fiume fiasco is bizarrely beached among the cypresses. In a hangar are a biplane that flew over Vienna in the war, vehicles that took part in the Fiume debacle, and the Italian flag. The mausoleum, where Fiume casualties are buried, features D'Annunzio's kitsch, self-aggrandising tomb, and, displayed in an eerie museum, his death mask.

Yachts at Salò

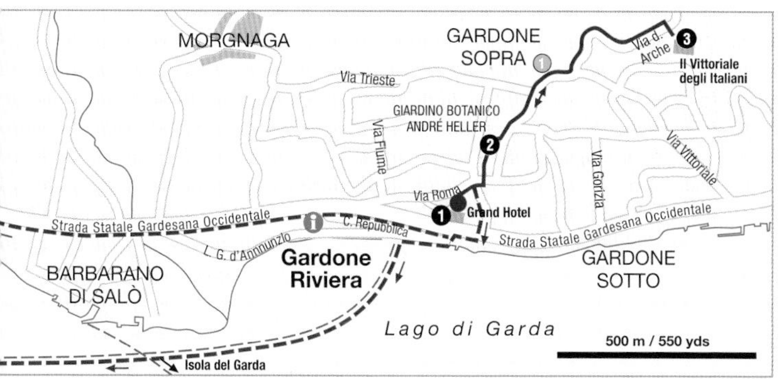

Lunch options

For lunch the **Agli Angeli**, see ①, is a good family-run restaurant, handy for Il Vittoriale; or, if cash is no consideration, head for the **Villa Fiordaliso** (see page 122). After lunch, drive or take the ferry to Salò.

Salò

Set on a beautiful deep bay with a long lakeside promenade, **Salò** is an appealing combination of bustling local town and elegant resort. It was founded in Roman times, then in 1337 became the capital of the Magnifica Patria, a community of 42 towns. During a less fortunate episode of its history, Salò was the seat of Mussolini's puppet republic in 1943 – his last desperate attempt to reorganise Fascism in Italy. A town of fleeting moods rather than awesome sights, it wears its history lightly. After an earthquake in 1901 the resort was rebuilt in airy Art Nouveau style and is still graced by elegant villa-hotel restaurants. One of the loveliest is the Villa Isabella, now the Hotel Laurin (Viale Landi 9) one-time headquarters of the Italian Foreign Ministry, presided over by Mussolini.

Stroll along the **Lungolago Zanardelli** ❹ (the lakeside promenade). The waterfront near the centre has some fine arcaded buildings, including the **Palazzo della Magnifica Patria**, the 17th-century town hall.

The most prominent landmark of Salò is the lofty campanile of the late Gothic **Duomo** ❺ (www.parrocchiadisalo.it; free) on the waterfront towards the eastern end of the Lungolago Zanardelli. The church has an elaborate Gothic altarpiece and a number of Renaissance paintings.

For lunch or dinner in Salò, try the **Osteria dell'Orologio**, see ②, or **Osteria di Mezzo**, see ③.

Emmental cheese at the market

Cobbled shopping street

TOUR 17
A taste of Trentino

Riva del Garda is Trentino's gateway to Lake Garda, and the castles of Arco, Drena, Toblino and Tenno are all a short drive away. Riva's picturesque location and healthy climate drew the European aristocracy from the early 1800s. Today it is a popular tourist resort.

DISTANCE: 60km (37 miles)
TIME: A leisurely day
START/END: Riva del Garda
POINTS TO NOTE: If lunching at Castel Toblino (Toblino Castle), be sure to make a reservation.

Riva del Garda

If arriving in Riva by car, park near the castle, ideally in the car park by the waterfront, the Giardini di Porta Orientale, or the adjoining Congress Centre.

As a medieval port for powerful prince-bishops, **Riva del Garda** ❶ became a pawn in the dynastic struggles between such city states as Milan, Venice and Verona. In 1703, during the War of the Spanish Succession, the port was sacked by the French, leaving Riva a shadow of its former self. Like the rest of Trentino, Riva was revived under Austrian rule (1815–1918), and it flourished as a fashionable resort, attracting such Mitteleuropean literary heavyweights as Franz Kafka, Thomas Mann and Friedrich Nietzsche. Contemporary Riva draws large numbers of tourists: middle-aged people off-season, and, in summer, a younger crowd who enjoy the watersports as much as the culture.

Wine country

Thanks to its microclimate, Garda Trentino is favourable to wine-growing, and vineyards are abundant. The most noteworthy grape is the Nosiola, which produces dry white wines and Vino Santo Trentino. The latter is a sweet dessert wine made with grapes that are dried out on wooden racks and then pressed during Holy Week, before being aged for three years in oak casks.

Rocca di Riva

Begin your tour of Riva at the lakeside **Rocca**, the moated medieval castle upon which the resort is centred. This austere military

Riva del Garda

stronghold, which once included an arsenal, barracks and palace, evokes only a partial sense of its former glory. The Rocca was designed as a fortress, but the Renaissance prince-bishops of Trento turned the interior into a patrician residence. It was further domesticated during Austro-Hungarian times, when its fearsome appearance was compromised by the lowering of its corner towers.

Beyond the drawbridge, the **Riva del Garda Museo** (Piazza Cesare Battisti; www.museoaltogarda.it; charge) has a minor art collection, sculptures from regional churches and archeological finds going back to the Bronze Age.

Piazza Cavour

After the Rocca, you might hit a lakeside café, or, from the adjoining Piazza Garibaldi, take Via Mazzini to **Piazza Cavour**, the main inland square, which is often obscured by market stalls. Here, you can buy local olives, cheese and wine at the Wednesday market; for excellent coffee, head for Bar Pasticceria Maroni.

Piazza 3 Novembre

Return to the Rocca and head west to the main **Piazza 3 Novembre**, which opens onto the lake. The square is lined with 15th-century Venetian-Lombard palaces, including the town hall. With its 13th-century gateway, a view of the 16th-century bastion above, and **Hotel Sole**, once an Austro-Hungarian rulers' residence, the square is a microcosm of Riva's history. The hotel has lost much of its grandeur, but its sunny terrace is good for drinks.

For spectacular views over the lake, take the lift up the **Torre Apponale** (www.museoaltogarda.it; charge). The tower has previously served as a prison, a store for salt and grain, and as a look-out point during World War I. Still today, it makes a great spot for people-watching.

Windsurfer on Lake Garda

Torbole

When you are ready to leave Riva, set off east along the main SS240 for 4km (2.5 miles) to **Torbole** ❷. Presenting the less genteel face of Lake Garda, what was once a fishing village is now a lively watersports centre that benefits from unusual wind conditions. Just before midday, the Ora southern wind whips down the lake and fills the sails of windsurfers until early afternoon.

If lunch is now a priority, you could try the Trentino specialities at Torbole's **Piccolo Mondo**, see ①, by the River Sarca, or, if you fancy lunch in Castel Toblino, start driving north following signs for Arco and Trento.

Alternatively, the footpath from Riva to Torbole (4km/2.5 miles) along the waterfront affords fine lake and mountain views. Goethe described Torbole as 'a wonder of nature, an enchanting sight'. The setting is as alluring as ever, but the village is rather spoilt by the main coastal road slicing through. However, this is no deterrent to hikers, free climbers, paragliders, windsurfers or sailing enthusiasts who descend on Torbole all year round.

Arco

After 5km (3 miles) you come to **Arco** ❸, a spa once favoured by Austro-Hungarian grand-dukes, and renowned for its gardens and pleasant climate. In the late 1800s, the resort was characterised by *belle époque* balls, health cures and carriage rides.

The former archducal gardens overlook the wizened stump of the **Castello di Arco** (www.trentino.com/en/highlights/castles/castello-di-arco; charge), which looms above the resort. A steep path winds up to the castle, but the interior, for all its fragments of Gothic frescoes depicting courtly scenes, does little justice to the striking setting.

Drena and Toblino castles

Continuing 18km (11 miles) north to Toblino, you will see on the right (beyond Dro) **Castello di Drena** (www.trentino.com/en/highlights/castles/castel-drena; charge). The stark late-12th-century castle, controlling the Sarca and Cavedine valleys, was destroyed in 1703, but has undergone restoration in recent years. Today it serves as a venue for exhibitions and conferences. A museum contains local archeological finds.

Castel Toblino ❹ (www.casteltoblino.com), set on the tiny lake of the same name, and with an atmospheric restaurant, seems to materialise from nowhere. Diners at the **Ristorante Castel Toblino** (see page 121) can visit the atmospheric interior, complete with Renaissance courtyard and 17th-century stoves. Others can enjoy a coffee or glass of wine in the bar/café below, with a lovely terrace overlooking the lake.

Arco Castle

Adamello-Brenta Park

Retrace your path to Sarche and take the first right turn – towards Comano Terme. The start of this western route skirts the **Parco Adamello-Brenta**, named after the Brenta rock formations, a Dolomite group marked by towering limestone pinnacles and surfaces bathed in a pink-tinged orange sheen. Toblino's vineyards give way to neat barns and lush Alpine pastures, deep forests and sheer rock faces.

The road to Riva

Comano Terme ❺ is a thriving spa resort, with its curative waters gushing out of the rocks at 28°C (82°F). Next head for **Bleggio Superiore** ❻ (5.5km/3.5 miles), a rambling village in a lovely Alpine setting, well-signed from Comano Terme.

From Bleggio follow the signs for **Fiavè** ❼ (5km/3 miles), which has an **archeological site** mired in the bogs just outside the village on the Riva road and the **Museo delle Palafitte di Fiavè** (www.cultura.trentino.it; charge), dedicated to prehistoric pile dwellings. The nature reserve features the remains of a late Neolithic village.

Continue on the Riva road (the SS421) to **Lago di Tenno** ❽ (11.5km/7 miles), a lake formed by a landslide. The medieval village of **Tenno** ❾ clustered around a private castle, lies 3km (2 miles) to the south.

From here, the road twists down to Riva del Garda. On the approach to Riva, the reappearance of olive groves represents the clearest shift back to the sultry Mediterranean microclimate of Lake Garda.

Food and Drink

① Piccolo Mondo
Via Matteotti 108, Torbole;
www.hotelpiccolomondotorbole.it
This family-run hotel restaurant serves typical Trentino fare – game, dumplings, mushrooms, polenta and apple strudel – as well as Mediterranean cuisine. €€

② Al Volt
Via Fiume 73, Riva del Garda,
www.ristorantealvolt.com
In the elegant little rooms of a historic palazzo, you can try Trentino specialities with a modern twist or fish fresh from the lake. Extensive wine list. €€

Dinner in Riva

For dining options in Riva del Garda, you could choose one of the restaurants overlooking the illuminated Rocca, or **Al Volt**, see ②, north of Piazza 3 Novembre. Alternatively, the **Restel de Fer** (see page 121), between Riva and Torbole, is well worth the walk (1.6km/1 mile) or short drive from the centre.

Cycle race through the streets of Arco

WALK 18
Milan

The dynamic business and design capital of Italy presents the perfect urban antidote to the languid atmosphere of the lakes. On this day excursion, explore the Duomo, indulge in designer shopping and stroll by night in the arty Brera quarter or lively Navigli.

DISTANCE: Minimum 3km (2 miles) on foot
TIME: A full day
START: Piazza del Duomo
END: Brera quarter
POINTS TO NOTE: From Como, Stresa, Bergamo or Varese, a direct train journey takes about an hour. From the Stazione Centrale, Milan's main rail station, catch the metro to the Duomo (cathedral). Consider booking a night at the opera (www.teatroallascala.org). A viewing of *The Last Supper* should also be booked well in advance (see page 100).

The lure of Milan for most visitors is the chance to indulge in designer shopping in Italy's fashion citadel. Further temptation comes in the form of culture on an international scale, from the Duomo to opera at La Scala to Leonardo's *The Last Supper*. The historic city centre is easily manageable for visitors, and the distances between the cathedral and the designer shopping district are walkable.

The Duomo

Piazza del Duomo is dominated by Europe's largest Gothic cathedral, the **Duomo** ❶ (www.duomomilano.it; charge). The capacity is around 40,000 people, and the façade is adorned by 3,000 statues, 135 spires and 96 gargoyles. This unfinished masterpiece was begun in 1386, and seamlessly blends Gothic, Baroque, Neoclassical and neo-Gothic styles. French-style flying buttresses and soaring pinnacles contrast with the excessive width preferred by native builders. Do not miss going up to the ***terrazzi*** (roof terraces), either by lift or (slightly cheaper) by clambering up 158 steps. For access to both, go to the back of the Duomo. Apart from fine views of the city and, on very clear days, as far as the Matterhorn, you can admire the gilded figure of the sacred **Madonnina**, the city's protector, soaring over Gothic spires.

'The Last Supper' by Leonardo da Vinci

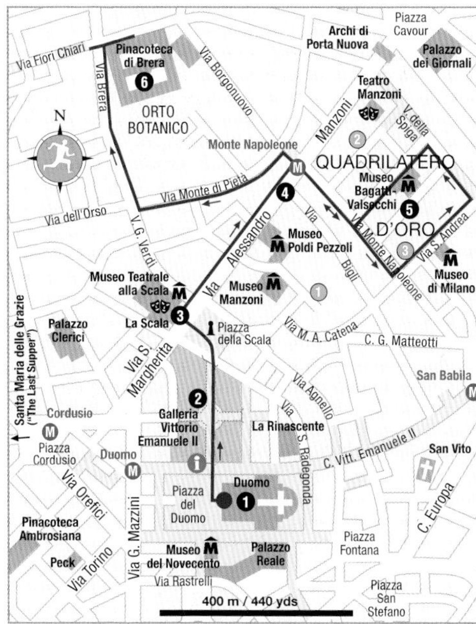

La Rinascente

Just off the square, **La Rinascente** (Via Santa Radegonda 3), the city's most upmarket department store, makes a possible first port of call for shopping. Its panoramic rooftop restaurant, **Le Terrazze**, overlooks the spires of the cathedral. If food shopping is on the agenda, then head for **Peck** (Via Spadari 9), a gastronomic temple west of the cathedral.

Galleria Vittorio Emanuele II

Connecting Piazza del Duomo with La Scala opera house is the **Galleria Vittorio Emanuele II** ❷, a splendidly arcaded shopping gallery and rendezvous known as *il salotto di Milano* (Milan's front parlour).

Among the restaurant/bars here, **Savini** (www.savinimilano.it) has been welcoming stars from La Scala since 1867, a fine place for afternoon tea or an *aperitivo* if you don't feel like the full formal dining experience. Among the Galleria's best bars is the Art Nouveau Zucca **in Galleria** (www.camparino.com) at no. 78 (the Duomo end). It is a classic spot for an *aperitivo* – especially a Campari, as Davide Campari, the inventor of the drink, was born here on the first floor. Those with a sweet tooth should not miss Marchesi1824 , a branch of one of the city's historic *pasticcerie*.

La Scala

The Galleria leads to Piazza della Scala, home to **La Scala** ❸, Italy's most celebrated opera house, which reopened at the end of 2004 after a lengthy, and controversial, refurbishment. A visit to the

The Last Supper

Somewhat out on a limb geographically, Milan's single most famous sight is Leonardo da Vinci's exquisite painting of *The Last Supper*, known to the Italians as Il Cenacolo. It 'hangs' on the refectory wall of the church of Santa Maria delle Grazie (Piazza Santa Maria delle Grazie 2; booking in advance obligatory, follow links from the official website www.cenacolovinciano.org). Book well ahead to guarantee a viewing slot. To protect the fresco, only thirty visitors are allowed in at any one time, and the visit is limited to fifteen minutes.

Museo Teatrale alla Scala (www.teatroallascala.org; charge), which traces the history of opera and theatre in the city, allows you to peep into the fabulously opulent interior.

Museo PoldiPezzoli

You won't have time for many museums on a day trip to Milan, but this one is a real gem – and not too big. You will pass it en route from La Scala to the fashion shopping district. The **Museo Poldi Pezzoli** (Via Manzoni 12; www.museopoldipezzoli.it; charge) contains an exquisite collection of Renaissance paintings, antiques and curios that belonged to Gian Giacomo Poldi Pezzoli, who owned the palace in the 19th century. On his death, he stipulated that the building and its contents should be accessible to the public.

Quadrilatero d'Oro

From Piazza della Scala, head northeast along **Via Manzoni** ❹ towards the world-famous shopping quarter. If it's time for lunch and you want to follow in the footsteps of Verdi, Donizetti and Toscanini, divert to the **Antico Ristorante Boeucc**, see ①, by taking the first turn on the right, leading to Piazza Belgioioso. Another Milanese institution is **Bice**, see ②, further on, in the heart of the fashion district.

The so-called **Quadrilatero d'Oro** ❺ (Golden Quadrangle) is defined by Via Manzoni, Via Monte Napoleone, Via della Spiga and Via Sant'Andrea, home to all the big fashion designers. At the intersection of Via Monte Napoleone and Via Sant'Andrea, call in at the **Pasticceria Cova**, see ③, one of the few family-run shops that have survived the ever-increasing rents in the quarter.

After a reviving coffee, cross over Via Manzoni for Via Monte di Pietà and take the second street on the right for **Via Brera**.

The Brera

Formerly the city's artisan district, this is a chic, picturesque area, with art galleries and alternative bars still providing a colourful hint of the bohemian.

Galleria Vittorio Emanuele II

Food and drink

1 Antico Ristorante Boeucc
Piazza Belgioioso 2, www.boeucc.it
The oldest restaurant in Milan, offering classic Milanese cuisine within a fabulous late-17th-century palazzo. Dishes such as saffron-flavoured *risotto alla milanese* and chateaubriand with béarnaise sauce are served with practised formality. €€€€

2 Bice
Via Borgospesso 12, www.bicemilano.it
This is a classic spot for both Milanese risotto and celebrity spotting in a bustling atmosphere. If you don't fancy risotto, there are plenty of interesting and innovative options ranging from artichoke salad with parmesan or crab with oil and lemon to chestnut gnocchi with pesto. €€€€

3 Pasticceria Cova
Via Monte Napoleone 8, www.pasticceriacova.com
An elegant, historic *pasticceria/caffè*, ideal for a coffee-and-cake break while you are shopping in the Quadrilatero d'Oro. Specialities are *Sachertorte* (chocolate cake) and *panettone* (the light Milanese Christmas cake, nowadays eaten at any time of year). The cappuccino is heavenly too, and it is also a lovely place to come for a spritz or prosecco and nibbles at *aperitivo* hour. €

Brera Art Gallery

The quarter is home to Milan's showcase museum, the **Pinacoteca di Brera** 6 (www.pinacotecabrera.org; charge), with one of the finest collections of Italian masterpieces. The collection spans some six centuries and includes works by Mantegna, Giovanni Bellini, Tintoretto, Veronese and Caravaggio.

Nightlife

If you decide to spend the evening in Milan, you'll find an array of options to suit any preference. The liveliest streets in the centre are in the Brera – **Via Brera** and **Via Fiori Chiari**, both of which are popular for an evening stroll. Via Fiori Chiari fills with fortune tellers and illegal street traders selling fake designer goods as night falls. Alternatively, sample the nightlife of the trendy **Navigli** canal quarter, southwest of the centre (Porta Genova metro).

If you are enamoured by the fashion district, then slink into the bar at the Four Seasons Hotel (Via Gesù 6/8). Set in a frescoed former monastery, this is a glamorous place for an early evening *aperitivo.*

Catwalk in Italy's fashion capital

Duomo roof terraces

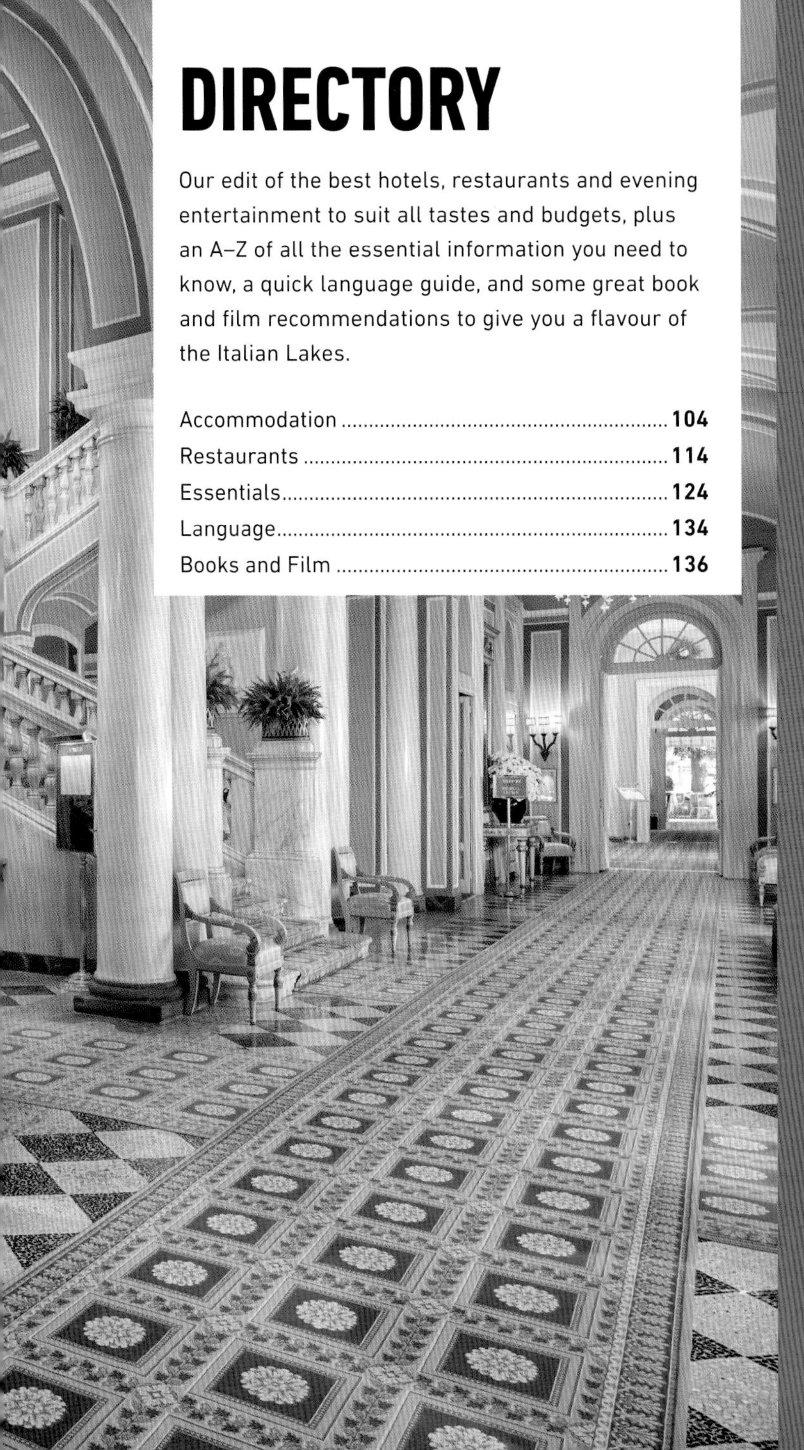

DIRECTORY

Our edit of the best hotels, restaurants and evening entertainment to suit all tastes and budgets, plus an A–Z of all the essential information you need to know, a quick language guide, and some great book and film recommendations to give you a flavour of the Italian Lakes.

Accommodation **104**
Restaurants **114**
Essentials **124**
Language **134**
Books and Film **136**

Accommodation

Accommodation on the lakes is abundant, with grand dowager hotels on the waterfront, romantic retreats in the hills, farmhouses, city-centre designer hotels, and self-catering villas and apartments. Accommodation is not cheap, especially if you choose a lakeside location. Hotels are categorised from one to five stars and five-star deluxe; the stars refer to facilities rather than quality.

Seasonal variations

Many of the lake hotels are closed between October and March. In high season (which varies according to each hotel but includes Easter and can go all the way from May through to September), hotels with a restaurant may insist on half-board with stays of no less than three days. Provided you know the hotel has a decent restaurant, half- (or full) board can be very good value.

Agriturismi

Working farms, converted barns or other rural properties that rent out rooms or apartments are known as *agriturismi*. These are an excellent choice for exploring rural regions, and for active holidays such as walking, fishing and cycling. Some *agriturismi* offer breakfast and an evening meal based on home-grown produce. Details of properties are available on www.agriturist.it and www.agriturismo.net.

Price categories

Price guide for a double room for one night with breakfast:

€€€€ = over €300
€€€ = €200–300
€€ = €100–200
€ = below €100

Tourist tax

The Tassa di Soggiorno, tourist tax varies from region to region and depends on the star rating of the hotel. The tax is levied on a maximum number of nights, which can be anything from four to ten (i.e. after the maximum number of nights, you no longer pay). Young children are usually excluded. If you have prepaid your hotel bill the tax will not have been included (or mentioned) – it is always charged when you check out at the hotel. B&Bs and residences are also included, usually at a slightly lower rate.

Lake Maggiore

Relais Villa Porta

Via A. Palazzi 1, Luino, http://relaisvillaporta.com

A late-18th-century villa, built on a hunting estate on the shores of Maggiore and set in a large park with romantic trails and a waterfall. It has prettily decorated guest rooms, a restaurant specialising in lake fish and a private beach. Two terraces

The imposing Grand Hôtel des Borromées

make the most of the lake views. Three suites are also available. €€€€

Grand Hotel des Iles Borromées & Spa

Corso Umberto I, 67, Stresa, www.borromees.com

Stresa's grande dame, this historic waterfront hotel faces the Borromean Islands. The *belle époque* decor is very lavish indeed, at times overwhelmingly so. Many of the luxury rooms have fabulous views of the lake and Alps. Facilities include palm-shaded gardens, indoor and outdoor swimming pools, a wonderful spa and fitness centre, tennis courts, a helipad and a landing stage for private boats. €€€€

Grand Hotel Majestic

Via Vittorio Veneto 32, Verbania, www.grandhotelmajestic.it

Another historic hotel, built in 1870, this great lady was favoured by artists from Debussy to Toscanini. Most rooms have panoramic views of the lake, while the wellness centre offers Ayurvedic and beauty treatments. There are lush gardens, a pool and a small sandy beach too. Apartments with access to hotel facilities also available. €€€€

Hotel Garni Millennium

Via Dogana Nuova 2, Locarno, www.millennium-hotel.ch

Once Locarno's customs house, today this handsome building is a small hotel with simple rooms. The best of the twelve rooms has a lake view. Friendly, helpful staff. €€

Lido

Viale Libertà 11, Angera, www.hotellido.it

An engaging villa-hotel with a private beach and good fish restaurant (see page 37). The guest rooms are peaceful and functional. €€

Pironi

Via Marconi 35, Cannobio, www.pironihotel.it

A gem of a hotel, housed in a converted medieval Franciscan monastery. Original features, such as frescoes, vaulted ceilings and medieval columns, have been retained, and guest rooms are all individually furnished with antiques. The old cellars have been transformed into an inviting wine bar. €€€

Il Porticciolo

Via Fortino 40, Laveno, www.ilporticciolo.com

A scenic four-star hotel on the lake with views of the Alps across the water. The rooms are comfortable, and there is a fine panoramic fish restaurant that serves lake fish, trout ravioli and scampi risotto. €€€

Il Sole di Ranco

Piazza Venezia 5, Ranco, www.ilsolediranco.it

Situated 4km (2.5 miles) north of Angera, this peaceful four-star villa-hotel has a graceful, restful style, lush grounds and lakeside views. Although

Grand Hôtel des Borromées reception desk

the emphasis here is on the gourmet restaurant (see page 115 , the hotel has pleasant rooms, including luxury suites with lake views. A swimming pool, hammam and sauna overlooking the water add to the attractions of this long-established inn. €€

Villa Aminta

Via Sempione Nord 123, Stresa, www.villa-aminta.it

This ravishing little Art Nouveau hotel was built by an Italian admiral in 1918. Gourmet fare, lavish rooms (see page 115), a spa and fitness centre and views overlooking the pool and lake are all on the menu. €€€€

Lake Orta

La Bussola

Via Panoramica 24, www.hotelbussolaorta.it

Set in an elevated position, this welcoming family-run hotel has stupendous views over the lake and across to the Isola San Giulio. The rooms are simple but charming, and the superior rooms have views of the lake. There is an outdoor swimming pool in the gardens and a panoramic terrace restaurant. On-site parking. €€

Hotel Aracoeli

Piazza Motta 34, www.ortainfo.com

This very central little hotel is minimalist and quirky. Each of the seven rooms is individually designed – with futons, waterfall showers with transparent walls and breathtaking views of the lake. Very good breakfasts. There is parking up the hill. €€

Hotel Cortese

Via Due Riviere 24C, www.cortesehotel.it

Standing at the foot of Monte Mottarone, this 4-star hotel has spectacular views of the surrounding hills, woodland and the lake. Rooms are well equipped and of a good size. There is an open-air swimming pool. €€

Leon d'Oro

Piazza Motta, Orta San Giulio, www.albergoleondoro.it

A family-run hotel with a romantic setting on the waterfront, overlooking the island of San Giulio. The standard bedrooms are small but bright and airy, many with good views. See page 50 for information on its restaurant. €

Piccolo Hotel Olina

Via Olina 40, www.piccolohotelolina.eu

Charming little hotel with fresh, modern rooms scattered around the historic centre. Rooms come without views of the lake but represent excellent value. Very good breakfast buffet. There is parking available up the hill. €€

Villa Crespi

Via G. Fava 18, Orta San Giulio, www.villacrespi.it

This grandiose Moorish folly, built by a 19th-century cotton merchant, has atmospheric public rooms as well as personalised bedrooms with original parquet floors, canopied beds and

The view from Villa Aminta

Villa Crespi

whirlpool baths. The cherry on the cake is the lovely three-Michelin-starred restaurant with sophisticated cuisine (see page 116). €€€€

Varese

Art Hotel

Via Bertini 3, Viale Aguggiari 26, www.arthotelvarese.it

Charmingly converted into a small hotel, this Biumo palazzo, at the foot of the Sacro Monte, within easy walking distance of the city centre, has a lovely garden, bar and sitting room. The rooms are simply but stylishly furnished with a light and understated contemporary touch (shower but no bath). Breakfast is excellent, and the small restaurant makes good use of local ingredients. Highly recommended. €€€

Bologna

Via B. Broggi 7, Varese; www.albergobologna.it

A welcoming three-star family-run hotel in the heart of the Old Town, with simple, spacious rooms. Attached is a fine trattoria with specialities from Emilia Romagna, including pasta, salami and antipasti. €

Hotel di Varese

Via Como 12, www.hoteldivarese.com

This hotel in Varese's historic centre is set in a beautiful Liberty villa. Its 21 rooms are furnished, modern and functional. Breakfast is taken in the attractive breakfast room or in the garden. €€

Palace Grand Hotel Varese

Via L. Manara 11, Varese, www.varese.ipalazzihotels.com

An Art Nouveau palace set on Mont Campigli, with gorgeous views across the city, lake and hills. The public rooms have a ponderous charm, while suites are spacious. There is a haute-cuisine restaurant here, plus gardens, tennis courts, a swimming pool and gym. €€

Lake Como

Bellavista

Piazza Bonacossa 2, Brunate, www.bellavistabrunate.com

A luxury suite at Villa Aminta

The spa at Villa Aminta

The outdoor pool at Grand Hotel Villa Serbelloni

This Art Nouveau boutique hotel in the hilltop village of Brunate lives up to its name and has stupendous views of Como and the Alps. As well as the beautiful views, it is a peaceful spot, with a panoramic restaurant, garden and wellness area; the funicular down to Como is just 50 metres (164ft) away. €€

Le Due Corti

Piazza Vittoria 12/13, Como, www.hotelduecorti.com

This former monastery and post house has been sensitively converted, despite the pool being placed in what were once the cloisters. The mood is one of quiet good taste, with warm fabrics and exposed beams matched by cosy rooms and a good restaurant. €€€

Florence

Piazza Mazzini 46, Bellagio, www.hotelflorencebellagio.it

A charming traditional hotel that has been in the same family for over 160 years. Public rooms feature a mix of burnished wood panelling and contemporary furniture; bedrooms are warmly inviting and priced according to views. There is a good restaurant, a cocktail bar with a lakeside terrace and a small spa with whirlpool bath, sauna and hammam. €€€

Garden

Via Armando Diaz 30, Nobiallo di Menaggio (about 1.5km/1 mile north of Menaggio), www.hotelgarden-menaggio.com

A rarity – an inexpensive family-run B&B, in a small villa on the shore of Lake Como. It has twelve plain and simple rooms, a very pretty garden and a beach area for guests. €

Grand Hotel Menaggio

Via IV Novembre 77, Menaggio, www.grandhotelmenaggio.com

A four-star lakeside hotel with panoramic views and well-equipped bedrooms. The service is good, and facilities include two restaurants, a terrace, bar, heated pool, gardens, private moorings for boats, water-skiing equipment and parking. €€€€

The view of Villa D'Este from the Mosaic Garden

Grand Hotel Tremezzo

Via Regina 8, Tremezzo, www.grandhoteltremezzo.com

Close to Villa Carlotta on the western shore, this is one of the lake's finest hotels. Built in 1910, it is furnished in Art Nouveau splendour, and offers sumptuous period rooms and terraced grounds dotted with modern sculptures. Facilities include three restaurants, a pizzeria and a bar, three swimming pools (one with a breath-taking view of the lake), a spa, yoga studio, private beach and marina. €€€€

Villa d'Este

Via Regina 40, Cernobbio, www.villadeste.com

The undisputed empress of the lake, this sumptuous 16th-century villa has been a hotel since 1873 and features palatial frescoed rooms studded with antiques. Facilities abound, with a luxury spa, lake-floating pool, indoor pool, golf, watersports, eight tennis courts, squash courts, a gym, sauna and Turkish bath and private boats. This has long been a retreat for the rich and famous, from J.F. Kennedy to Alfred Hitchcock to Madonna. €€€€

Grand Hotel Villa Serbelloni

Via Roma 1, Bellagio, www.villaserbelloni.com

An utterly charming luxury hotel comparable with Villa d'Este, with a wealth of marble, crystal chandeliers and frescos. With two restaurants (one Michelin-starred), three bars, a state-of-the-art health spa, outdoor pool, private beach, watersports and tennis, it has everything you could want, plus superb lake views. €€€€

Locanda Sant'Anna

Via Per Schignano, Argegno (Como), www.locandasantanna.it

A truly wonderful rural retreat in the hills above Argegno, this family-run inn was once a retreat for Como clergy. There are eight comfortable rustic rooms, one suite and a recommended restaurant (see page 117). €€

Bergamo

Gombit Hotel

Via Mario Lupo 6, www.gombithotel.com

Next to the medieval Torre del Gombito, this was the first designer hotel in the upper town. Modern and stylish, the rooms are individually decorated in a palette of restful neutrals, typically with exposed brick stonework or timbers and pastel-coloured furnishings. €€

Petronilla Hotel

Via San Lazzaro 4, www.petronillahotel.com

Behind a stately façade right in the heart of the city, the interior of this intimate boutique hotel surprises, its vibrant modern interior wittily pairing reproductions of famous works of art, cool designer furnishings and zesty pops of colour. Service is top-notch; prepare to be pampered. €€€

Villa D'Este Cardinal Suite

Villa D'Este Sundeck Bar

Lake Iseo

Albergo Bellavista

Siviano, Monte Isola, www.albergo-bellavista.it

Set on Monte Isola, this is a small, friendly, hotel with unfussy, tasteful modern rooms, terrace and views over the village. Free pick-up and taxi service on arrival and depature. €

Araba Fenice

Via Caproni 246, Località Pilzone d'Iseo, (2.8km/1.75 miles northeast of Iseo), www.arabafenicehotel.it

A good-value four-star hotel, with fabulous lake views and an excellent restaurant that serves Lombard cuisine and fish specialities, and decent breakfasts too. Nearly all the rooms have views, and there is a sunny terrace for meals or drinks in fine weather. €€

I Due Roccoli

Via Silvio Bonomelli Est, Località Invino di Sotto, Iseo, Polaveno www.idueroccoli.com

A delightful old villa hotel set in the hills 7km (4.5 miles) from Iseo. Low-key elegance is the keynote, with terracotta floors, exposed fireplaces and airy rooms. The noted restaurant features panoramic views, and its specialities include fresh lake produce, home-made salami and fine Franciacorta wines. €€

Relais Mirabella

Via Mirabella 34, Clusane, www.relaismirabella.it

In the hills above Clusane, this four-star converted country hotel enjoys panoramic views of Lake Iseo. Rooms are light and stylish. There is a good restaurant with a terrace, swimming pool and gardens. €€€

Riva Lago

Via Cadorna 7, Sulzano, www.rivalago.it

This elegant hotel with a pale blue classical façade enjoys an idyllic setting right on the lake, just a ferry hop away from the island of Monte Isola. Guest rooms are cream-coloured, light and airy, breakfasts are lavish affairs by the lakeside, the pool is lovely and the bar offers delicious Franciacorta sparkling wines by the glass. €€

Franciacorta

L'Albereta

Via Vittorio Emanuele II, Erbusco, www.albereta.it

Set in Franciacorta wine country, this striking ivy-covered villa among the vineyards is a favourite among gourmets and wine buffs. As well as a pool, tennis and spa centre, wine-tasting trips are available. €€€€

Azienda Agricola

Al Rocol, Via Provinciale 79, Ome, www.alrocol.com

Wine estate and farm with simple but tasteful bedrooms and apartments on a family-run estate producing award-winning Franciacorta wines, olive oil, honey and grappa. €

Cappuccini Convento

Via Cappuccini 54, Cologne Franciacorta, www.cappuccini.it

L'Albereta

Set on a hilltop overlooking Franciacorta, this 16th-century former monastery is now a gracious inn, restaurant and small spa – although walking the lovely grounds is equally therapeutic. Wine-tasting, elegant restaurant (using fresh produce from the monastic orchards and vegetable gardens), old-world bedrooms and spa. €€€

Relais Franciacorta

Via Manzoni 29, Colombaro (Franciacorta), www.relaisfranciacorta.it

Popular 17th-century farm estate converted into elegant rural hotel. It's a peaceful spot with large grounds and views towards Lake Iseo. The bedrooms are spacious, and there is a good restaurant. €€

Villa Gradoni

Frazione Villa, Monticelli Brusati (8km/5 miles from Iseo), www.villafranciacorta.it

A rural *agriturismo* run by the Bianchi family, who produce sparkling, red and white Franciacorta wines. The self-contained flats are roomy and comfortable, with exposed beams and stonework. €

Lake Garda

Ca' del Baldo Agriturismo Relais

Via Cappuccini 32, Caprino Veronese, www.cadelbaldo.com

A delightful *agriturismo* with four apartments in restored farm buildings near the foot of Monte

L'Albereta spa

Baldo. With a heated pool, gym and the possibility of cycling, horse-riding and many other excursions as well as the lake nearby, this is an ideal place for a family holiday. €

Color Hotel

Via Santa Cristina 5, Bardolino, www.colorhotel.it

The fresh, modern design of this hotel makes interesting use of colour and light. The rooms are spacious with balconies, a variety of bars and lounges and there are several pools in the gorgeous gardens. E-bicycles, mountain bikes, canoes and SUPs for rent. €€€

Suite at L'Albereta

Room at the Grand Hotel Fasano

Duomo

Lungolago Zanardelli 63, Salò, www.hotelduomosalo.it

Named after the nearby cathedral, the hotel has a fine setting on Salò's spacious waterfront, good-value guest rooms and an excellent restaurant – a magical place to sit on the lakeside terrace on a summer's evening. €€

Gardesana

Piazza Calderini 5, Torri del Benaco, www.gardesana.eu

Given it has hosted the likes of Churchill, Laurence Olivier, Maria Callas and King Juan Carlos I of Spain, this traditional hotel is delightfully low-key, and the rooms are reasonably priced. The harbour side setting is enchanting. Well thought of restaurant with a gorgeous setting. €€

Grand Hotel Fasano

Corso Zanardelli, 190, GardoneRiviera, www.ghf.it

Once a hunting lodge, this opulent five-star hotel has lush grounds and old-world grandeur. Luxurious guest rooms vary in size and are priced accordingly. Along with gourmet cuisine, there is a stylish spa, indoor pool and private lakeside beach. €€€€

Laurin

Viale Landi 9, Salò, www.hotellaurinsalo.it

This sumptuous Art Nouveau villa, set in gorgeous lake-view grounds, served as the Ministry of Foreign Affairs during Mussolini's puppet regime. A fine restaurant is the setting for high-class cuisine. Rooms are comfortable, stylish and understated. €€€

Locanda San Vigilio

Punta San Vigilio, www.locanda-sanvigilio.it

With one of the most beautiful settings on the lake, this tiny hotel has only seven rooms, four superior rooms and three suites each with a country house feel; specify if you want a lake view, as not all have balconies. It also has an excellent *terrazza* (terrace), where you can dine alfresco in a perfect romantic setting. For extra privacy, ask for the Limonaia, reached through Italy's oldest lemon grove. Arrive by boat for added panache. Booking advised. €€€€

Le Palme

Via Porto 36, Limone sul Garda, www.lepalmelimone.com

The lakeside restaurant at Villa Fiordaliso

Set beside the ferry landing stage, this 17th-century waterfront hotel is in a quaint but touristy resort. It has a small pool, a rooftop sun terrace, a restaurant, bar and a panoramic whirlpool. €€

Hotel Querceto

Via Panoramica 113, www.hotelquerceto.com

Perched up on Monte Baldo above the town, with spectacular views, this cosy little mountain inn offers the best of all worlds, with 22 rooms, a terrace and pool, sauna and, bar and restaurant, its own glorious botanical gardens, and a transparent dome for forest bathing (or a cup of tea). It is just a short distance from the cable-car, you can swing down to town and the lake-shore. Closed Oct– beginning of Apr. €€

Villa Cortine Palace Hotel

Viale C. Gennari 2, Sirmione, www.palacehotelvillacortine.com

A romantic luxury hotel set in parkland a few minutes' walk from the crowds of Sirmione's historic centre. The Neoclassical villa has landscaped gardens with fountains, a pool, tennis courts, watersports, a private jetty with sun-loungers, boats to rent and a path to a beach restaurant. €€€€

Villa Fiordaliso

Corso Zanardelli 132, Gardone-Riviera, www.villafiordaliso.it

An exclusive Art Nouveau villa hotel where Mussolini and his mistress Clara Petacci once stayed. It has a beautiful lakeside setting and a richly decorated interior, but the highlight is perhaps the restaurant with waterside terrace (see page 122). €€€€

Milan

Antica Locanda Leonardo

Corso Magenta 78, www.anticalocandaleonardo.com

A stylishly restored, idiosyncratic hotel where chic minimalist rooms feature the occasional carefully chosen antique or splash of colour and a pretty inner courtyard and garden for breakfast or drinks. Popular with the fashion crowd. €€

Antica Locanda dei Mercanti

Via San Tomaso 8, www.locanda.it

This charming boutique hotel has the cosiness of an old-fashioned inn. Some rooms have rooftop views and terraces. €€€€

Bulgari Hotel

Via Privata Fratelli Gabba 7B, www.bulgarihotels.com

On the edge of the Botanical Gardens, the Bulgari Hotel has been designed with the precision and opulence that is the trademark of the name. Four figure room rates. €€€€

Gran Duca di York

Via Moneta, 1, www.ducadiyork.com

Close to the Duomo, this is a boutique hotel has lovely light rooms, some with stylishly planted private terraces. It is housed in a stylish 18th-century palazzo. €€€

Breakfast terrace at Laurin

The view from a suite at Hotel Laurin

Restaurants

This wealthy part of Italy has more than its fair share of restaurants, from tiny, intimate spots to a cluster of grand Michelin-starred affairs, so you will certainly not be short of a place to eat. Many ingredients are locally sourced, with excellent lake fish. The most difficult part is simply deciding where to dine. Opening times are generally lunch *(pranzo)* 12/12.30pm–2/3pm and dinner *(cena)* 7.30/8pm–10pm. In main towns and resorts, restaurants may stay open later – this is often the case with pizzerias (most of which open evenings only). Menus at lunchtime are frequently cheaper and lighter than those offered in the evening.

Price categories

Price guide for a two-course à la carte dinner for one with half a bottle of house wine:

€€€€ = over €80
€€€ = €50–80
€€ = €25–50
€ = below €25

Lake Maggiore

Grotto Sant'Anna

Via Sant'Anna 30, Cannobio, 0323-70682

Along the Cannobina Valley, in the mountains behind Cannobio, this restaurant perches on the edge of the Orrido di Sant'Anna, a spectacular gorge with a beautiful waterfall. The simple menu features delicious meat dishes, excellent pasta, cheeses and home-made desserts. Wild mushrooms are available in the autumn months. The restaurant is about 10km (6 miles) from Cannobio, and you can hike, bike or go by car. €€

Lo Scalo

Piazza Vittorio Emanuele III 32, www.loscalo.com

The most refined of Cannobio's restaurants, plum on the waterfront piazza. The building is lovely, a 14th-century palazzo with an atmospheric portico, and the cuisine is classic Piemonte fare with innovative touches; crispy veal sweetbreads, or beef carpaccio and foie gras, for example, followed by seared tuna or veal cheek. The menu changes daily. €€–€€€

Milano

Corso Zannitello 2, Pallanza, www.ristorantemilanolagomaggiore.it

Sophsticated cuisine with the occasional nod to Japan, making the most of fresh fish, local meat and home-grown vegetables, served on a lovely terrace overlooking the lake. The home-made pasta is wonderful, and presentation is exquisite. Tasting menus if you want to push the boat out. €€€€

Villa Aminta restaurant

Osteria del Centenario

Viale Verbano 17, Locarno, http://osteriacentenario.ch

One of Locarno's finest gourmet restaurants. Fresh local ingredients are used to create dishes such as risotto with lake fish bottarga and gold leaf, quail with fermented melon, and bison fillet. Tasting and set lunch menus. €€€€

Il Piccolo Lago

Via Filippo Turati 87, Verbania Fondotoce, Lago di Mergozzo, www.piccololago.it

On the lakeshore road in Mergozzo, this is a top-class two-Michelin-starred restaurant with fabulous lake views. Intriguing menu created by chef Marco Sacco. A lovely unpretentious interior complements the views. The Gourmet Boat experience is a marvellous idea – you are given an electric-powered boat and picnic, and three hours to go wherever you like, at either lunch or evening. Details on the website. €€€€

Ristorante Il Vicoletto

Vicolo del Poncivo 3, www.ristorantevicoletto.com

This charming little family-run restaurant serves up imaginative, well-presented dishes – try the tasty mussels and salmon curry. Due to its small size, booking is essential, particularly if you want to eat at one of the handful of outside tables. €€

Il Sole di Ranco

Piazza Venezia 5, Ranco, www.ilsolediranco.it

Founded in 1850 by the Brovelli family, the restaurant is now run by Davide Brovelli who fuses tradition and modernity with a light touch – a spritz of lime to lift a summer seafood spaghetti dish, a dab of kefir to add zing to a risotto of tomato, basil, lemon and thyme oil. The award-winning restaurant sits right on the lake, with an arbour for summer dining. Dishes are elegantly presented and served. It is also a hotel with fourteen rooms. €€€

Il Vicoletto

Vicolo del Poncivo 3, Stresa, www.ristorantevicoletto.com

Tucked away in an alley off the main square, this is a tiny restaurant where the focus is on good ingredients, home cooking and a dash of creativity – delicious pasta and simple roast or grilled meat and fish. €€

Lo Stornello

Via Cavour 35, Stresa, www.ristorantelostornellostresa.it

An intimate restaurant with tables neatly packed together in a dining area featuring light grey walls and wine bottles encased in small niches. The food is particularly good, with Mediterranean specialities such as lake fish balls and cod with red onions and bell pepper sauce. €€

Villa Aminta

Via Sempione Nord 123, Stresa, www.villa-aminta.it

This villa is a delightful five-star luxury hotel with two alluring restaurants: the large richly decorated Le Isole

Le Isole's dining room, Villa Aminta

with a candlelit terrace, which serves light lunches and gourmet set-menu dinners, and the enchanting à la carte Restaurant Mori. Both have gorgeous lake views, encompassing the Borromean Islands, and are justifiably sought after for weddings and private parties. €€€€

Lake Orta

Al Boeuc

Via Bersani 28, Orta San Giulio, 0339 584 0039

Sample a good glass of wine or two accompanied by prosciutto, cheese or *bagna cauda* (crudités in hot olive oil, garlic and anchovy dip). This is the oldest and one of the most atmospheric taverns in town. €

Al Sorriso

Via Roma 18, Soriso, www.alsorriso.com

This gastronomic Mecca in the tiny village of Soriso, 8km (5 miles) south of Orta San Giulio, attracts devotees from all over Europe for inspirational Piedmont and Mediterranean cuisine, produced by chef Luisa Valazza. This is a family-run affair, with an elegant, friendly atmosphere (*sorriso* means 'smile' as well as being a play on the name of the village), but be prepared for arm-and-a-leg category prices unless you opt for the 'business' lunch menu (three courses plus dessert or cheese but no drinks) served Wed, Thurs and Fri. There are also eight comfy guest rooms, should you choose to stay. €€€€

Villa Crespi

Via G. Fava 8/10, Orta San Giulio, www.hotelvillacrespi.it

An imaginative blend of Alpine and Mediterranean flavours, presented in the sumptuous surroundings of a Moorish-style villa that is now a hotel with a wonderful restaurant. Feast on Sicilian scampi, carnaroli rice with clams and thyme, Piedmont veal, sea bass with oysters and caviar –accompanied by a fine French or Italian wine from their superb cellar. €€€

Lake Varese

Vecchia Riva

Via G. Macchi 146, Schiranna, Lago di Varese, www.vecchiariva.com

Choose a fine day and sit in the garden, looking out onto the peaceful waters of Lake Varese. This hotel restaurant serves up a fine spread of antipasti (where you can help yourself buffet-style), and a daily changing menu. Risotto (as you might expect from its proximity to Italy's main rice growing area) is a speciality. €€€

Lake Como

Acquadolce

Via Regina Vecchia 36, Carate Urio, www.ristoranteacquadolce.it

This place enjoys a stylish modern setting right on the lake, sporting an enticing waterfront terrace. Home-made pasta, lake fish, salads and decadent desserts are elegantly presented and served. €€€€

View of the Grand Hotel Villa Serbelloni in Bellagio

Il Cavatappi

Via XX Settembre, Varenna, www.cavatappivarenna.it

'The Corkscrew' is a minute eatery, with just five tables, hidden in an alley off the main piazza of Varenna. The cuisine is simple but delicious, the atmosphere cosy and the wine cellar well stocked. The owner-cum-chef will talk you through the local lake specialities. Booking advisable. €€

Il Gatto Nero

Via Montesanto 69, Cernobbio, www.ristorantegattonero.it

Rub shoulders with celebrities (this is one of George Clooney's favourites), gaze down onto great lake views, and feast on fish and meat specialities. The 'Black Cat', perched in the hills above Cernobbio, is sumptuously decorated and has soft, mellow lighting and a romantic atmosphere. The setting alone is worth a detour. €€€€

Locanda Sant'Anna

Via Sant'Anna 152 (on the Schignano road), Argegno, www.locandasantanna.it

A rural retreat in the hills above Argegno. Local mountain dishes such as home-made whole-wheat pizzocheri with cabbage, potatoes and fontina cheese, potatoes and mushrooms soufflé with dried beef, venison with blueberries, salami and Alpine cheeses are served in two adjacent rooms, with a garden setting, and valley and lake views. €€

Mistral

Grand Hotel Villa Serbelloni, Via Roma 1, www.villaserbelloni.com

The fine restaurant of this grand hotel produces highly sophisticated and intricate Mediterranean dishes using meticulously sourced ingredients. Eat in a wood-panelled restaurant, evocative of the great lake steamers, or on the lakeside veranda. Prices are high even for the Lakes – for most people this is very much a special occasion restaurant. €€€€

Teatro

Piazza Verdi 11, Como, www.caffeteatrogonzaga.it

In the heart of Como, on a piazza facing the Duomo, this is a stylish café and bistro in the same building as the historic Sociale Theatre. The café is open all day and evening, the bistro, with simple contemporary cuisine, for lunch and dinner. Tables are laid out on the square for alfresco dining in summer. Also a nice spot for an evening aperitivo. €

Vecchia Varenna

Contrada Scoscesa 14, Varenna, www.vecchiavarenna.it

Managed by the Castiglioni family since 1987, restaurant Vecchia Varenna, is located in the historic part of town. Amid an irresistible waterside setting, with Lake Como and mountain views, Vecchia Varenna serves fish and meat, pasta, rice meals and tasty desserts. They also run evening cooking classes followed by dinner. €

The lake view at Mistral

A luxurious carpaccio at Mistral

Villa d'Este

Via Regina 40, Cernobbio, www.villadeste.com

Hotel Villa d'Este has three restaurants and two bars. The setting is a palatial 16th-century villa amid luxuriant gardens at Cernobbio. Formal Italian *haute cuisine* is served at the Veranda (jackets and ties are required in the evening), while The Grill, underneath the plane trees in summer, and Il Platano – where diners can choose among eight exquisite dishes each accompanied by the perfect wine – are more informal. €€€€

Bergamo and Franciacorta

Baretto di San Vigilio

Via Castello 1, San Vigilio, Bergamo, www.barettosanvirgilio.it

At the top of Bergamo's San Vigilio funicular, you can sit out on this romantic restaurant's terrace (in summer), enjoying gourmet fare and wonderful views of the Città Alta below. The menu offers a wide selection of home-made dishes. You might start with an *antipasti* or home-made pasta, follow with meat or fish, and finish off with one of their famous desserts. There are also 250 wines to choose from. €€€

Cantina e Agriturismo Al Rocol

Via Provinciale 79, Ome, Franciacorta, www.alrocol.com

This rustic inn is located on a family-run wine estate and farm. Brescian and Franciacorta dishes served here include *casonsèi* (ravioli with bacon and melted butter), tagliatelle with wild mushrooms, beef with local olive oil, and, in autumn and winter, *polenta e osei*, the 'Brescian lunch' of spit-roasted pork and chicken on polenta. Award-winning wines, olive oil, honey and grappa are all available to buy. At times may be open to residents only, so check in advance. €

Al Donizetti

Via Gombito 17a, www.donizetti.it

Located in what was formally a cheese market, this pleasant bar with seating on a breezy shaded portico offers tasty cheese and cold-cut platters that go down a treat with a glass of one of the many wines on offer. Choose from goat's cheeses, prosciutti crudi, Bresaola, salumi d'oca (goose) and more. €€

Da Franco

Bartolomeo Colleoni 8, Bergamo, www.dafrancobergamo.org

Located next to the beautiful and historical Piazza Vecchia, Da Franco is one of the best restaurants in Bergamo's upper town. Pizza too in the evenings. €€

Punta dell'Est

Via Ponta 163, Clusane, www.ristorantehotelpuntadellest.it

The homely fish restaurant of this welcoming family-run hotel is the place to eat mixed grilled lake fish or baked tench with polenta. It has a wonderful setting right on the lake by the ferry landing stage. €€

Grilled salmon at Villa D'Este

Baretto di San Vigilio

Relais I due Roccoli

Via Silvio Bonomelli, Loc. Invino di Sotto, Iseo, www.idueroccoli.com

This romantic hilltop eyrie above Iseo is a great place for fresh lake fish. The dining room has views over the lake, and there is a courtyard for summer dining by candlelight. Also a hotel. €€

Relais Mirabella

Via Mirabella 38, Clusane, www.ristorantedanadia.com

Located high up, 1.5km (1 mile) southwest of the centre of Clusane, with a lovely romantic terrace, this oasis of peace and elegance has wonderful views over the lake. Creative cuisine, with the focus on fish and seafood, is cooked with panache and presented with a flourish and has won chef Nadia Vicenzi a Michelin star. €€€

Restaurant LeoneFelice Vista Lago

L'Albereta Hotel, Via Vittorio Emanuele 23, Erbusco, www.albereta.it

A sublime restaurant with a modern Italian design in a dreamy setting. The kitchen of Fabio Abbattista – the executive chef – offers a menu made with excellent ingredients. All meals are accompanied by great wines, mainly from the finest Franciacorta estates. Booking is essential. €€€€

Roof Garden

Hotel Excelsior San Marco, Piazza della Repubblica 6, www.roofgardenrestaurant.it

The top (eighth) floor of this four-star hotel hosts an expensive haute cuisine restaurant. Expect international fine dining, nouvelle-style (tiny portions, creatively presented) in contemporary surroundings with spectacular views of the floodlit walls of the old town. An open-air terrace runs around the exterior. €€€

Trattoria del Muliner

Via San Rocco 16, Clusane, www.trattoriadelmuliner.it

Clusane on Lake Iseo is famous for *tinca al forno* (baked tench) and this inviting, family-run trattoria is one

Platano restaurant at Villa D'Este

of the best places to try it, along with other tasty local specialities such as smoked trout and fish soup. €€

La Vineria

Via X Giorante 4, Brescia, www.lavineriabrescia.it

An authentic wine bar and inn that makes a nice place to stop if you happen to call in to the town of Brescia. Excellent cold cuts and cheeses as well as hot dishes. Informal but informed tasting advice is offered on good regional wines. €

Lake Garda

Agriturismo Trenta

Via Mazzane 2, Moniga del Garda, www.agriturismo30.com

A delightful *agriturismo* with a vine-covered terrace that overlooks the herb gardens and lake. The table d'hôte food is delicious, plentiful and affordable. Many of the ingredients, including fruit, vegetables, wheat flour and pasta, are produced on the farm. Booking essential. €€

Caffè Italia

Piazza Malvezzi 19, Desenzano del Garda, www.ristorantecaffeitalia.it

At this well-established café in the centre of the town you can enjoy anything from a morning cappuccino and croissant at the bar, a light lunch on the terrace, or a blow-out seven-course *menu degustazione* (tasting menu) in its fish restaurant. The fish is excellent, and includes French oysters, Sicilian scampi, sea bass and raw fish. This is also a fashionable spot for cocktails and liqueurs. Vegetarian options too. €€€

Esplanade

Via Lario 10, Desenzano del Garda, www.ristorante-esplanade.com

Outstanding cuisine and a panoramic lake setting combine to make this one of the most desirable formal restaurants in the region. The menu is seasonal and thee dishes sophisticated, inventive and beautifully presented. Excellent wine list. €€€€

Gatto Moro

Via Giotto 21, Borghetto di Valeggio sul Mincio, www.ristorantegattomoro.it

Traditional meals with simple, fresh ingredients. A good choice if you are in the mood for grilled beef or pork and roast potatoes. €€

Pasticceria Vassalli

Via di San Carlo 84-6, Salò, www.pasticceria-vassalli.it

Specialising in chocolate, sweets and cakes, this café/*pasticceria* is hard to resist. Among the local favourites are *pan di Salò*, a rich cake made with candied peel and limoncello, a version of the liqueur made from Lake Garda lemons. €

Il Porticciolo

Lungolago Marconi 22, Lazise, www.ilporticcioloristorante.it

An inviting family-run lakeside restaurant that serves a vast array of fish and

Castel Toblino is an enchanting place to have a meal

vegetable *antipasti*, fresh lake and sea fish and a tempting selection of *risotti*, with citrus-spiked lake fish, with prawns and green peppercorns or with radicchio and local Monte Veronese cheese. €€

Restel de Fer

Via Restel de Fer 10, Riva del Garda, www.resteldefer.com

Restel de Fer is a delightful rustic *locanda*, which has been run by the Meneghelli family since 1400 and is known for dishes such as *trout carpaccio with fennel and elderflower* or marinated char salad. Closed for refurbishment at the time of writing but due to reopen in 2024. €€€

Risorgimento

Piazza Carducci 5–6, Sirmione, www.risorgimento-sirmione.com

A centrally-located restaurant, with tables on a piazza with views of the lake. Some really interesting dishes you won't find anywhere else – giant ravioli stuffed with hare, butter herbs and Bagoss cheese, foie gras risotto with sour butter (a local speciality), black garlic and walnuts. Very popular, so booking by phone is obligatory (030 916325). €€€

Ristorante Castel

Localita, Castel Toblino,1, Sarche, www.casteltoblino.com

A romantic castle on the enchanting Lake Toblino, where the inventive local fare features some very unusual ingredients – caper powder, yuzo, beech-scented oil. Highlights include duck with caramelised peach and traditional canderdoli dumplings with chanterelles and Puzzone di Moena cheese. €€€

Ristorante Re Lear

Piazza Cavour 23, Malcesine, 045-740 0616

Ranked as one of the top restaurants in Malcesine, the King Lear offers innovative combinations. Menus change monthly, and vegetarian, vegan and gluten-free meals are available. The restaurant is in the heart of the Old Town, a stone's throw away from Castello Scaligero, with a terrace on Piazza Cavour. €€€

La Rucola 2.0

Via Strentelle 3, Sirmione; www.ristorantelarucola.it

Recently renovated and redecorated, this is a Michelin star restaurant located close to the castle. The creative Mediterranean cuisine includes a wide choice of seafood and meat plus a huge wine selection. Reservations are compulsory for dinner and advisable for lunch. €€€€

La Terrazza

Via Benaco 14, Torbole; www.allaterrazza.com

The broad lake-view veranda and the inspired regional cuisine make this one of the most appealing restaurants in the northern part of Lake Garda. With ingredients sourced from the lake, specialities include chub meatballs, perch salad, lake sardines and risotto with tench. Wash your meal down with a crisp Pinot Grigio or Muller Thurgau. €€

La Tortuga

Via XXIV Maggio 5, Gargnano; www.ristorantelatortuga.it

This intimate little restaurant in the historic centre of Gargnano serves exquisite dishes and great wines. Fish (both lake and sea) predominate, but you can also find vegetarian *antipasti* and main courses, such as scallops with a zucchini sauce and mint oil or sea bass fillet with Franciacorta and cocoa beans. There is a range of tasting menu options and a well-stocked wine cellar. €€€€

Villa Feltrinelli

Via Rimembranze 38, Gargnano, www.ristorantevillafeltrinelli.com

This lakeside retreat, built in 1892, was home to Mussolini during World War II, and today is a luxury hotel with a cerebral gourmet restaurant with two Michelin stars. Lunchtime is à la carte only, evenings tasting menu only. One of the most expensive restaurants in the Lakes. €€€€

Villa Fiordaliso

Corso Zanardelli 132, Gardone Riviera, www.villafiordaliso.com

This small and stylish Art Nouveau villa-hotel right on the lake is where Mussolini stayed with his mistress Clara Petacci during the Salò republic. A lunch of ravioli with Bagoss cheese and dried pear, and roast grouper with caper butter and asparagus, followed by a stroll through the grounds is hard to beat. €€€€

Milan

L'Anima Del Gusto

Via dei Fontanili 2; www.lanimadelgusto.eu

Restaurant offers a friendly atmosphere and delightful seafood dishes. Try tuna tartare with Bronte pistachios and avocado, tagliolini with swordfish and bottarga and grilled swordfish with fennel and orange salad. Somewhat off the beaten track – but worth the taxi fare. €€

El Brellin

Vicolo dei Lavandai, Alzaia Naviglio Grande 14, www.brellin.com

Probably the most glamorous old washhouse ever. This 18th-century laundry, now an idyllic waterfront restaurant on the Naviglio Grande, has an evening menu of rich home-made pastas and Lombardy specialities such as creamy Milanese risotto. The locals love the evening cocktails and aperitivo buffet. €€

Cracco

Via Victor Hugo 4, www.ristorantecracco.it

Opened by the famous Italian chef Carlo Cracco, this gastronomic wonder was awarded one Michelin star for high-quality cooking. Specialities include fish soup crust and yolk marinated with asparagus and black truffle, saffron risotto and grilled bone marrow. There is also a café for coffee, light lunches, drinks and exquisite pastries. €€€€

Milan's Navigli canal quarter

Villa Feltrinelli

La Dogana del Buongusto

Via Molino delle Armi 48, www.ladoganadelbuongusto.it

Warm and welcoming family-run restaurant serving exceptional cuisine in a rustic interior with cavernous, exposed brick walls, wooden ceilings and old-world knick-knacks. The hearty cold cut platters include wild boar and deer ham, and the menu includes some excellent Milanese dishes. The 30cm meat brochette served with baked potato and herb-flavoured butter is a must. €€

Gelateria Marghera

Via Marghera 33, Fiera; www.gelateriamarghera.it

Join a queue that stretches around the block for the best ice cream in Milan. This gelateria has an overwhelming array of flavours to choose from – plus delicious semifreddo and meringue cakes. Heaven on a hot day and definitely worth the wait. It is not central, but close to Angeli and Wagner metro stations. €

Joia

Via Panfilo Castaldi 18, www.joia.it

Joia specialises in vegetarian haute cuisine and was the first vegetarian restaurant in Europe to be awarded a Michelin star. The setting is simple and contemporary, the clientele hip, the presentation unique. The cuisine is avant-garde and capricious. The Michelin star means high prices, but the set lunch menus are good value. Book at least one week ahead. €€€€

Langosteria

Via Savona 10, www.langosteria.com

This atmospheric restaurant with an understated interior serves some of Milan's best fish and seafood dishes. The oyster bar is the perfect spot for a pre- or postprandial drink, while seating is in a series of individually furnished rooms featuring maritime ornaments, including an upturned boat. The Catalan-style King Crab is superb, as is the scampi tartar with foie gras. Its sister-restaurant, Langosteria Bistrot (Via Bobbio 2), offers similar cuisine in a more informal setting. €€€–€€€€

Luini

Via Santa Radegonda 16; www.luini.it

Very handy for a quick snack by the Duomo, this famous bakery specialises in *panzerotto*, a freshly made Puglian pastry €

Dining by Lake Garda

Essentials

Age restrictions

The age limit for consuming and purchasing alcohol in Italy is 18. Stricter penalties on establishments selling to those under 18 have been enacted. The minimum age for driving, provided you hold a full licence, is 18 but for renting a car in most cases a driver must be 21 or over.

Budgeting

The best-value hotels and restaurants tend to be located away from the lake fronts. In high season you can expect to pay €200–300 for a comfortable double room with bath, €100–200 in a simpler hotel or B&B. Count on €50–80 upwards for a three-course evening meal with half a bottle of wine in a restaurant, and €20 or so for a pizza and beer. Drinks and coffee taken at the bar are quite a bit cheaper than those at a table with waiter service. Entrance fees to museums, galleries and gardens range from a few euros to €20; entrance is free for EU citizens under 18 (but no longer for those over 65) and those from 18–25 normally get a fifty percent discount. Fuel costs are similar to those across Europe, but public transport remains inexpensive.

Business hours

Banks are generally open weekdays 8.30am–1.30pm and 3–4pm (afternoon opening times may vary). Banks at airports and main stations usually have longer opening hours and are open at weekends. **Shops** are traditionally open from Monday–Saturday 9am–1pm and 3.30/4–7.30pm, but an increasing number of stores, especially in cities and tourist resorts in high season, are open all day. Outside major resorts, many shops are closed on Sunday, and some also close on Monday morning.

Children

There is plenty to keep youngsters entertained on the lakes, from boat trips and cable-car rides to leisure parks and castles. Lake Garda is by far the best-equipped lake for families, with vast theme parks, water parks, and sandy beaches. Concentrated in a 25km (15.5-mile) radius in the southeast of Lake Garda, there are a number of major attractions.

Villa Pallavicino

Lake Maggiore's Stresa may be a rather sedate resort, but children can be kept entertained by ferry rides and a visit to Villa Pallavicino. The extensive gardens are home to animals, exotic birds and a children's playground. In summer, a mini train provides a shuttle service between the park and Stresa's centre.

Lake Garda is the best equipped for families

Child-friendly attractions and activities

Thousands of holidaymakers descend annually to the shore north of Peschiera del Garda, home to **Gardaland** (www.gardaland.it; charge), Italy's number one theme park. It boasts over forty Disney-styled attractions and forty shows.

Situated 4km (2.5 miles) to the north is CanevaWorld and its Movieland Studios (www.caneva world.it; charge), which comprises the fun-filled Acqua Water Park and film-themed attractions.

The most exciting rides in the region are the Monte Baldo cable-car (see page 89), providing panoramic views of the astonishing landscapes (see page 39).

Water parks and gardens

The **Parco Cavour** near Valeggio sul Mincio (www.parcoacquaticocavour.it; charge) provides plenty of aquatic entertainment. The **Parco Giardino Sigurtà** (www.sigurta.it; charge) at Valeggio sul Mincio features aquatic gardens, with fish-filled ponds, a toy railway, and nature trails.

Climate

Spring, summer and autumn are all good times to visit the lakes, not least due to the fine weather conditions. Ideal months are May, June and September when it is warm and sunny but not as hot or croweded as midsummer. April and May are the best months for the blooming of camellias, azaleas and tulips.

The climate can be unpredictable due to differences in altitude and microclimates. In Milan, temperatures can soar in summer to well above 30°C (86°F) and the humidity is high – hence the exodus of Milanese to the cooler lakes. October and November are the wettest months in the region but usually include quite a few unexpectedly fine days. Winter tends to be foggy and cold, and is best avoided.

Crime and safety

The lakeside resorts are generally very safe, as are most of the small towns. In Milan, keep an eye on possessions, especially in crowded places such as the Piazza del Duomo and train and bus stations. For insurance purposes, theft and loss must be reported straight away to the police station *(questura)*.

Customs

Free exchange of non-duty-free goods for personal use is allowed between EU countries. See guidance levels:

Tobacco: 800 cigarettes, or 400 cigarillos, or 200 cigars, or 1kg of tobacco.

Spirits: 10 litres above 22 percent strength or 20 litres below 22 percent strength.

Wine: 90 litres (only 60 litres can be sparkling).

Beer: 110 litres.

Lake Maggiore lights up at night

Those from non-EU countries should research their country's current complete list of import restrictions.

Electricity

Sockets take two-pin, round-pronged plugs; supplies are 220-volt. UK appliances require an adaptor, US ones a transformer.

Embassies/Consulates

If you lose your passport or need other help, contact your nearest national embassy or consulate.
Australia: Australian Consulate General www.italy.embassy.gov.au
Canada: Canadian Consulate www.canadian-consulate.com
New Zealand: Consulate General www.mfat.govt.nz
Republic of Ireland: Honorary Consulate, www.dfa.ie
UK: British Consulate General www.british-consulate.org
US: US Consulate General, http://it.usembassy.gov

Emergency numbers

Ambulance: 118
Fire: 115
General emergency: 112
Police: 113

Health

All EU countries have reciprocal arrangements for reclaiming the costs of medical services. UK residents and other non-EU members should have private travel insurance that covers medical care, emergency repatriation costs and additional expenses such as accommodation and flights for anyone travelling with you.

A pharmacy *(farmacia)* is a good first stop for medical advice. The name of the duty or all-night pharmacy is posted on pharmacy doors.

Internet

Most hotels, and an increasing number of cafes offer Wi-Fi which is available in airports, train stations and other public places but you will more often find yourself relying on 4G and 5G.

Left Luggage

There are left-luggage facilities at all the airports and at Milan's Central Station. Look for the signs '*Deposito Bagagli*'.

LGBTQ+ travellers

Milan is Italy's gay-friendly capital. The Italian gay organisation, Arcigay (www.arcigay.it) is a useful source of information, as is the *Rough Guide to Top LGBTQ+ Friendly Places in Europe*.

Lost Property

In the event of lost valuables contact the nearest police station *(questura)*.

Maps

Tourist offices can normally provide you with free town maps and sketchy regional ones. The Touring

Santa Maria Assunta church in Orta San Giulio

Club Italiano (TCI) publishes excellent road and hiking maps.

Media

Newspapers. English and foreign newspapers are available from kiosks of main towns and resorts. National newspapers include the Milan-based centre-right daily, *Corriere della Sera*, and its centre-left rival, *La Repubblica*.
Television and radio. Most hotels provide satellite TV, broadcasting 24-hour English-speaking news channels – but not necessarily many other channels in English. Some have streaming services. Italian TV, comprising the state-run RAI 1, 2 and 3 channels, along with a large number of private channels, churns out chat-shows, soaps, films and numerous advertisements. The state-run radio stations, RAI 1, 2 and 3, mainly broadcast news, chat and music. The easiest way of keeping in touch when travelling is to download the BBC Sounds app.

Money

Currency. The unit of currency in Italy is the euro (€), which is divided into 100 cents. Banknotes come in denominations of 500, 200, 100, 50, 20, 10 and 5 euros; coins come in 2 and 1 euros, and 50, 20, 10, 5, 2 and 1 cents.
Cash machines. ATMs are widespread and have instructions in the main European languages, though an increasing number of places accept contactless payments, so it is no longer necessary to carry wodges of cash around.
Credit cards. Major international credit cards are accepted in most hotels, restaurants, stores and supermarkets.

Police

In an emergency the *Carabinieri* can be reached on 112, or the Polizia dello Stato on 113.

Post

Post offices normally open Mon–Fri 8.35am–1.25pm, Sat 8.35am–12.35. Only main post offices in major towns open in the afternoons. Stamps *(francobolli)* can also be purchased from tobacconists.

Public holidays

Shops, banks, museums and galleries usually close on the days listed below:
1 Jan New Year's Day
6 Jan Epiphany
Mar/Apr Easter
Mar/Apr Easter Monday
25 Apr Liberation Day
1 May Labour Day
2 June Republic Day
15 Aug Assumption Day
1 Nov All Saints' Day
8 Dec Feast of the Immaculate Conception
25 Dec Christmas Day
26 Dec St Stephen's Day

Religion

Like the rest of Italy, the region is primarily Roman Catholic. The Church still plays a major role in

the community, although numbers of regular worshippers have been in decline for some years. Milan has congregations of all the main religions.

Smoking

Since 2005, smoking has been banned in indoor public places. This includes bars and restaurants, unless they have a separate area for smokers – which very few do.

Telephones

Phone numbers. Whether phoning from abroad or within Italy, the full area code including the 0 must be used. Toll-free numbers within Italy that begin 800 need no other code. Numbers starting with 0 are landlines, those starting with 3 are mobiles.
Calling from abroad. To dial Italy from the UK, dial 00 (international code) + 39 (Italy) + area code + number. To call other countries from Italy, first dial the international code (00), then the country code: Australia 61, Ireland 353, UK 44, US and Canada 1.
Mobile phones. UK mobile (cell) phones can be used in Italy, but check roaming rates with your provider before you leave – some charge no roaming fees for the first couple of weeks, but this varies and may change. It may be worth buying an Italian SIM card, available from any mobile-phone shop and many newsagents, if you intend to stay for a long time. The new small independent operators often have the best pay as you go deals – newsagents are usually well informed.

Useful numbers

Directory enquiries: 12
International enquiries: 176

Time differences

Italy is one hour ahead of Greenwich Mean Time (GMT). From the last Sunday in March to the last Sunday in October, clocks are put forward an hour.

Tipping

Tipping is not taken for granted in Italy, although a bit extra will always be appreciated. In restaurants five to ten percent is customary unless service has been added to the bill. For quick service in bars, leave a coin or two with your till receipt when ordering. Taxi drivers do not expect a tip but will appreciate it if you round up the fare to the next euro.

Toilets

Public toilets are hard to come by. If you use the facilities of cafés and bars, buying a drink will be appreciated – even if it is only a glass of mineral water at the bar.

Tourist information

Around Lake Maggiore

Stresa: www.stresaturismo.it
Varese: www.comune.varese.it

Windsurfer on Lake Garda

Around Lake Como

Bellagio: www.bellagiolakecomo.com
Como: www.visitcomo.eu
Menaggio: www.menaggio.com

Around Lake Iseo

Bergamo: www.visitbergamo.net
Iseo: www.visitlakeiseo.info

Around Lake Garda

Desenzano del Garda: www.desenzano.brescia.it
Gardone Riviera: www.rivieradelgarda.com
Riva del Garda: www.gardatrentino.it
Sirmione: http://visitsirmione.com

Milan

www.yesmilano.it

Tourist offices abroad

www.visititaly.com

Tourist board official websites

www.distrettolaghi.it – Lake Orta and the west of Lake Maggiore.
www.vareseturismo.it – province of Varese, including Lake Maggiore's eastern side.
www.ascona-locarno.com - Swiss Lake Maggiore.
www.turismo.regione.lombardia.it – Lombardy.
www.lakecomo.is – Lake Como.
www.bresciaholiday.com – Lake Iseo, Franciacorta, lower Lake Garda.
www.visitgarda.com – Lake Garda.
www.visitmilano.net– Milan.

Tours and guides

Tourist offices, travel agencies and hotels can provide details of tours and guides and excursions.

Transport

Arrival by air

For British travellers low-cost carrier Ryanair (www.ryanair.com) operates flights from London Stansted to Bergamo's Orio al Serio airport, easyJet (www.easyjet.com) and British Airways have regular flights from Gatwick and Heathrow respectively to Milan's Linate and Malpensa airports.

From the US there are direct flights to Milan from main cities, including New York, Miami, Atlanta, Los Angeles and San Francisco.

Airports

Malpensa. Located 50km (31 miles) northwest of Milan, Malpensa airport (www.milanomalpensa-airport.com) is a convenient arrival point for the lakes in the west of the region (Orta, Maggiore, Varese and Como). The airport's Terminal 1 is linked to Milan's Centrale, Garibaldi and Cardorna railway stations by the half-hourly Malpensa Express (www.malpensa express.it). Journey time to the centre is about forty minutes. The Malpensa Shuttle and Malpensa Bus Express provide regular coach services to Milan's Central Station, taking fifty to sixty minutes.

Santa Maria del Monte village

Linate. Situated 10km (6 miles) east of Milan, Linate (www.milanolinate-airport.com) is the closest airport to the city, and handles mainly domestic and European flights. The quickest and easiest way into the centre is by underground (Mon–Thurs 6am–10.30pm, Fri–Sun 6am–12.30am). There is also an hourly metro service through the night.

Orio al Serio. Bergamo's Orio al Serio airport, 48km/30 miles northeast of Milan (www.milanbergamoairport.it) is convenient for the western lakes, and ideal if you are heading to Lake Iseo. The city of Bergamo is only 5km (3 miles) away, with a bus service departing to the city every half an hour. Autostradale and Terravision operate half-hourly shuttle buses to Milan's Central Station, an hour away.

Valerio Catullo/Verona-Villafranca. Verona's airport (www.aeroportoverona.it) is 15km (9.5 miles) from Verona, and is handy for the Veneto shore of Lake Garda. Buses depart for Verona's rail station at 5.35am, 6.30am and then every twenty minutes until 11.30pm.

Other airports. Lugano airport (www.luganoairport.ch/en) is another useful gateway to the Italian Lakes, as are Venice and Treviso.

Arrival by rail

The journey from the UK to Milan, via Paris on Eurostar (www.eurostar.com) and the Frecciarossa to Milan or Verona takes just over seven hours to Milan. Milan and Como are well served by trains from Switzerland, Germany and France. If arriving from elsewhere in Italy, there are reliable connections from Turin, Bologna, Florence and Rome, and from within the lakes region. Detailed information on international rail routes can be found at www.seat61.com and www.thetrainline.com.

Arrival by car

The quickest route to Milan from the UK channel ports takes a minimum of twelve hours, over a distance of 1,040km (646 miles). For route planning and for details on the cost of petrol, road tolls levied on French and Italian motorways, and the Swiss motorway road tax, visit www.viamichelin.com. Reasonable motorways *(autostrade)* and main roads link the lakes from Turin, Milan, Como, Varese, Bergamo and Brescia. But bear in mind that the city centres and ring roads can be both confusing and congested.

Tolls are levied on the motorways, but it is worth the relatively small expense to cover ground fast. When you approach the payment barrier, make sure you choose the correct lane. Lanes marked 'Carte' will accept credit cards; cash lanes are indicated with a hand holding notes and coins.

Transport within the lakes region

Boats. Operating on all the main lakes, **ferries** *(battelli)* offer the most enjoyable and leisurely way of exploring the lakes. **Hydrofoils** *(aliscafi)* or **catamarans** *(catamarani)* are faster than ferries,

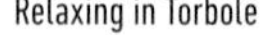
Relaxing in Torbole

but more expensive and less fun as passengers are confined to the inside. Tickets for these faster services allow use on ferries but not vice versa. On popular summer routes on the main lakes, the hydrofoils fill up quickly.

Useful **car ferries** *(traghetti)* link Intra and Laveno on Lake Maggiore; Menaggio, Varenna, Cadenabbia and Bellagio on Lake Como; and Toscolano-Maderno to Torri del Benaco and Limone to Malcesine on Lake Garda. **Timetables** covering all ferries and hydrofoils are available from ferry ticket offices, tourist information offices and online for the main lakes at www.navigazionelaghi.it. Timetables change at least twice a year, but the routes remain quite constant. Ferries normally run from 7am but stop quite early in the evening, and services between 12.30pm and 2.30pm are limited.

There is a bewildering variety of **tickets and deals** for the major lakes, so check the options before your first trip. These include an all-day ticket for parts or all of the lake, a single or return ferry ticket, and a ferry ticket that includes entry to (or a price reduction at) major sites.

An all-day ticket is the most convenient option if you are making several journeys on the same day. Generally, children under the age of four travel free, four- to twelve-year-olds are just over half-price. Over-60s from the EU nations are entitled to a twenty percent reduction on weekdays (with proof of identity). Return boat tickets (excluding catamarans or hydrofoils) tend to be valid for two days.

Lake cruises. All local tourist offices and hotels will have details of lake cruises, some of which include dinner, lunch or an *aperitivo* on board.

Motorboat taxis. Public ferry services stop early in the evening so if you want to dine in another resort, you should organise transport for the return trip. As you might imagine, private motorboats are generally far more expensive than land taxis. Some island restaurants might transport diners back to the mainland. If you are worried about being stranded, discuss the options with your restaurant – you may be able to share a taxi-boat with other diners. If you are using a motorboat taxi, negotiate a price before setting off.

Bus. A reasonably priced bus network links towns and villages along the lakeshores. If you do not have a car, a bus can be the quickest means of reaching some destinations; for example, from Stresa to Lake Orta, and (on Lake Garda) from Desenzano to Sirmione, Salò, Gardone or Limone – all of which are inaccessible by train. Services linking villages are less regular, and some stop very early in the evening.

Rail. Milan is the main rail hub for the lakes, with excellent, well-priced services to the main towns across the region. Bergamo, Stresa (Lake Maggiore) and Como (Lake Como) all take around an

Yachts on Lake Garda

Limone sul Garda

hour by rail. Lakes Varese and Garda (using the station at Brescia) are also well served by trains. Desenzano, on the Milan–Venice line, is the main terminal on the southern shore of Lake Garda. However, the lakes themselves are better served by ferries and buses.

Intercity, Eurocity or Eurostar trains levy a supplement of at least 30 percent and require seat reservations. It is advisable to make a reservation well in advance. Return tickets offer no saving on two singles. Tickets must be stamped in the yellow machines on the platforms before boarding the train. Tickets bought on the train incur a hefty supplement. For information on train travel in Italy, see www.trenitalia.com or www.trenord.it.

Land taxis. Taxi fares are high, and there are additional charges for luggage in the boot (trunk), trips at night and trips on Sundays and holidays. Beware of touts without meters who may approach you at airports (especially Linate) and large train stations. The main squares of the larger towns usually have a taxi rank.

Car rental

Car-rental bookings made in advance on using internet broker sites such as www.holidayautos.com or www.rentalcars.com work out cheaper than hiring on arrival. Make sure you check all the extras when comparing quotes. The major car-rental companies have offices in the main cities and airports. An ever-increasing number of companies have electric cars available. As for charging points, Italy is one of the best-supplied countries in Europe, with the roll out propelled by a joint initiative between Enel, the national electricity provider and Volkswagen. Lombardy is at the top of the list. To check charging stations, look at www.placetoplug.com.

Drivers must present their own national driving licence or one that is internationally recognised. There is an additional charge for an extra driver. Credit-card imprints are taken as a deposit and are generally the only form of payment acceptable. 'Inclusive' prices do not generally include personal accident insurance or insurance against damage to windscreens, tyres and wheels. Taking out private car hire insurance is always cheaper than getting it from the car hire companies. Reliable providers are www.questor-insurance.co.uk and insurance4carhire.com. You will have to pay any expenses up front, but you will be reimbursed.

Driving

Rules of the road. Drive on the right; pass on the left. Speed limits in Italy are 50km/h (30mph) in towns and built-up areas, 90km/h (55mph) on main roads and 130km/h (80mph) on motorways. Speeding and other traffic offences are subject to heavy on-the-spot fines.

At roundabouts the traffic from the right has the right of way. Seat belts are compulsory in the front and

A ferry awaits at Riva del Garda

back, and children should be properly restrained. The use of hand-held mobile telephones while driving is prohibited. The blood alcohol limit is 0.08 percent, and police occasionally make random breath tests. Lights must be used on motorways, dual carriageways and on all out-of-town roads. Visibility vests and a warning triangle are compulsory. **Breakdowns**. In case of accident or breakdown call 112 (general emergencies) or the Automobile Club of Italy (ACI) on 803116. The club has an efficient 24-hour service, which is available to foreign visitors. **Petrol**. On main roads there are plenty of 24-hour stations with self-service dispensers that accept euro notes but not necessarily credit cards. **Parking**. Finding a parking space in the centre of lakeside resorts is notoriously tricky. Check your hotel has parking facilities (charges can be quite high) or can recommend a parking lot nearby. Parking in towns is controlled by meters or scratch cards, available from tobacconists and bars. The larger towns have multi-storey car parks. Some free parking is controlled by parking discs (if you have hired a car a disc will be provided).

Travellers with accessible needs

Steep cobbled streets, steps and some museums without wheelchair access can present challenges for disabled travellers. Specialised tour operators can offer customised tours and itineraries, e.g. Limitless Travel (www.limitlesstravel.org). If you are going to be in Milan, visit the Milano per Tutti (Milan for All) website (www.milanopertutti.it) which provides a large amount of information for visitors with disabilities to the city.

Visas and passports

For citizens of EU countries, a valid passport or identity card is all that is required to enter Italy for stays of up to ninety days. Citizens of Australia, New Zealand, the UK, and the US also require only a valid passport. For stays of over ninety days a visa or residence permit is required.

Websites

Official tourist board websites:
www.distrettolaghi.it – Lake Orta and the west of Lake Maggiore.
www.vareseturismo.it – province of Varese, including Lake Maggiore's eastern side.
www.ascona-locarno.com – Swiss Lake Maggiore.
www.turismo.regione.lombardia.it – Lombardy.
www.lakecomo.is Lake Como. Weird address, but correct
www.bresciaholiday.com – Lake Iseo, Franciacorta, lower Lake Garda.
www.visitgarda.com – Lake Garda.
www.visitmilano.net– Milan.

Weights and measures

The metric system is used for all weights and measures in Italy.

Some roads are carved into the hillside

Language

Italian is relatively easy to pick up, if you have any knowledge of French or Spanish (or a grounding in Latin). Most hotels have staff who speak some English, and unless you go well off the beaten track, you should have little problem communicating in shops or restaurants. However, there are places not on the tourist circuit where you will have the chance to practise your Italian, and local people will think more of you for making an effort. Here are a few basics to help you get started.

Useful phrases

General

Yes *Sì*
No *No*
Thank you *Grazie*
Many thanks *Mille grazie*
You're welcome *Prego*
All right/That's fine *Va bene*
Please *Per favore/Per cortesia*
Excuse me (to get attention) *Scusi*
Excuse me (in a crowd) *Permesso*
Could you help me? (formal) *Potrebbe aiutarmi?*
Certainly *Ma, certo/Certamente*
Can you show me…? *Può indicarmi…?*
Can you help me, please? *Può aiutarmi, per cortesia?*
I need… *Ho bisogno di…*
I'm lost *Mi sono perso/a*
I'm sorry *Mi dispiace*
I don't know *Non lo so*
I don't understand *Non capisco*
Do you speak English/French/Spanish? *Parla inglese/francese/spagnolo?*
Could you speak more slowly? *Può parlare più lentamente, per favore?*
Could you repeat that please? *Può ripetere, per piacere?*
How much does it cost? *quanto costa?*
this one/that one *questo/quello*
Have you got…? *Avete…?*

At a bar/restaurant

I'd like to book a table *Vorrei prenotare un tavolo*
Have you got a table for…? *Avete un tavolo per…?*
I have a reservation *Ho prenotato*
lunch/supper *il pranzo/la cena*
I'm a vegetarian/vegan *Sono vegetariano/a vegano/a*
May we have the menu? *Ci dia la carta?*
What would you like? *Che cosa prende?*
I'd like… *Vorrei…*
mineral water fizzy/still *acqua minerale gasata/naturale*
a bottle of *una bottiglia di*
a glass of *un bicchieri di*
red/white wine *vino rosso/bianco*
beer *una birra*

Italians are easy-going

Numbers

One *uno*
Two *due*
Three *tre*
Four *quattro*
Five *cinque*
Six *sei*
Seven *sette*
Eight *otto*
Nine *nove*
Ten *dieci*
Twenty *venti*
Thirty *trenta*
Forty *quaranta*
Fifty *cinquanta*
One hundred *cento*
One thousand *mille*

Getting around

What time do you open/close? *A che ora si apre/chiude?*
Closed for the holidays *Chiuso per ferie*
Where can I buy tickets? *Dove posso fare i biglietti?*
What time does the train leave? *A che ora parte il treno?*
Can you tell me where to get off? *Mi può dire dove devo scendere?*
Where is the nearest bank/hotel? *Dov'è la banca/l'albergo più vicino?*
On the right *a destra*
On the left *a sinistra*
Go straight on *Va sempre diritto*

Online

What is the WiFi password? *Qual è la password WiFi?*
Is the WiFi free? *Il WiFi è gratis?*
Can I…? *Posso…?*
access the internet *collegarmi (a Internet)*
check e-mail *controllare le e-mail*
print *stampare*
plug in/charge my laptop/iPhone/iPad? *collegare/ricaricare il mio portatile/iPhone/iPad?*
How do I…? *Come…?*
connect/disconnect *ci si collega/scollega*
What's your e-mail? *Qual è la sua e-mail?*
My e-mail is… *La mia e-mail è…*

Health

Is there a chemist nearby? *C'è una farmacia qui vicino?*
sunburn *scottatura da sole*
sunburn cream *la crema antisolare*
insect repellent *l'insettifugo*
mosquitos *le zanzare*
antiseptic cream *la crema antisettica*

Social media

Are you on Facebook/Instagram/X? *È su Facebook/Instagram/X? (polite form) Sei su Facebook/Instagram/X? (informal form)*
What's your user name? *Qual è il suo nome utente? (polite form) Qual è il tuo nome utente? (informal form)*
I'll add you as a friend. *La aggiungerò come amico. (polite form) Ti aggiungerò come amico. (informal form)*
I'll follow you. *La seguirò su. (polite form) Ti seguirò su. (informal form)*

Practise your Italian at any opportunity

Locals will appreciate your effort to speak the language

Books and Film

The sight of slow steamers and snow-clad peaks stirs something deep in most visitors, but especially in the souls of poets. It is of little coincidence that two of the most romantic Roman poets, Virgil and Catullus, came from the lakes and were inspired by the seductive setting. Pliny, too, loved the lakes. Later, the Romantics fell in love with the region. 'This lake exceeds anything I ever beheld in beauty,' declared Shelley of Lake Como, exploring the lake in 1818. Novelist Edith Wharton, visiting in 1903, was intoxicated by the Romantic poets' visions of brooding lakes. The German poet and dramatist Goethe was drawn to Lake Garda by its classical resonance, even if it was the lemons rather than the literature that won his heart. 'What I enjoy most of all is the fruit,' he wrote in his journal in 1786. He had less fondness for Malcesine, where the Austrian police, spotting him sketching the castle, arrested him on suspicion of being a spy.

Since the 18th century, Lake Garda's summer villas have lured such luminaries as Byron and D.H. Lawrence. Lawrence said of Limone, 'as beautiful as the beginning of creation'. Ibsen and Vladimir Nabokov concurred, even if their preference was for the greater Gardone Riviera.

'One can't describe the beauty of the Italian lakes, nor would one try if one could,' wrote Henry James, on catching sight of Lake Maggiore. Few writers have taken the hint, and outpourings of purple prose, particularly from writers fleeing northern climes, are part of the lakes' legacy.

Books

Travel companions

Desiring Italy, Susan Cahill (ed). Writings by female authors (George Eliot, Edith Wharton, Muriel Spark, etc) on the beauty and culture of Italy.

Italian Days, Barbara Grizutti Harrison. A witty and eloquent look at Italy, revealing a fascinating insight into a nation.

History, society and culture

A History of Contemporary Italy: Society and Politics: 1943–1988, Italy and Its Discontents, 1980–2001 and Silvio Berlusconi: Television, Power and Patrimony, Paul Ginsborg. A masterly history of post-war Italy and its politics is completed with an account of the power of the country's most powerful politician.

Alps and Sanctuaries, Samuel Butler. The 18th-century traveller describes his journeys around the lakes.

Mussolini, Nicholas Farrell. A biography of the reviled Fascist dictator that pulls no punches.

Daniel Craig and Olga Kurylenko at the official presentation of the film "Quantum of Solace"

It includes the period of the Salò Republic, when Mussolini's powerbase was on the shores of Lake Garda.
The House of Gucci, Sarah Forden. A biography of Maurizio Gucci, the last family member to run the luxury-goods fashion empire.
The Dark Heart of Italy, Tobias Jones. Although flawed and obsessed with a Berlusconi era that is now history, this is an intriguing look at the underbelly of Italy, from politics, crime and (lack of) punishment to the Italian way of life.
How the English Made the Alps, Jim Ring. The English love affair with the Alps, from its beginnings in the early Romantic movement, through to its Victorian heyday.

Fiction and travelogue

A Farewell to Arms, Ernest Hemingway. The novel tells the story of a wounded American soldier in the Italian army who convalesces in Milan, inadvertently deserts while fleeing from the Germans but is reunited with his beloved in Stresa, on Lake Maggiore.
Europa, Italian Neighbours, A Season With Verona, Tim Parks. The novelist observes life in Italy in a series of light-hearted and affectionate tales.

Food and wine

Eating up Italy: Voyages on a Vespa, Matthew Fort. Exploring Italy's regions on an epic scooter trip, Matthew Fort paints a contemporary portrait of Italy through its food and the people who produce it.
Truly Italian, Ursula Ferrigno. An Italian cookbook with inspirational recipes and a vegetarian focus that features the healthiest northern Italian cooking.

Film

This beautiful area has inspired a number of films including:
A Month on the Lake (1995). This film, starring Vanessa Redgrave and Uma Thurman, is just one of many featuring Lake Como's magnificent Villa del Balbianello.
Star Wars Episode II: Attack of the Clones (2002). Villa del Balbianello features again, this time as planet Naboo, where the wedding of Anakin Skywalker (Darth Vader) and Padmé Amidala is held.
Ocean's Twelve (2004). George Clooney's attachment to Lake Como has led to films including this one, in which he stars, being filmed in the region. Villa Erba is used as the home of François Toulour, the Night Fox.
Casino Royale (2006). Parts of the acclaimed first James Bond film with Daniel Craig in the title role were filmed on Lake Como. Bond finds Mr White at his estate on the lake, Villa La Gaeta, and Villa del Balbianello is used as the sanatorium where Bond recuperates after being tortured by Le Chiffre.

The famous house used in the James Bond film "Casino Royale", on Lake Como

About This Book

The Pocket Rough Guide Walks & Tours series helps you discover the world's most exciting destinations through expert-curated itineraries: a range of walks and tours designed to suit all budgets, interests and trip lengths. These walks, driving tours and site excursions cover the destination's most classic attractions as well as a range of lesser-known sights, while food and drink stops for refreshments en route are highlighted in boxes. If you're not sure which one to pick, our Best Walks & Tours for... feature suggests which ones work best for particular interests. The Introduction provides a destination overview, while the Directory supports the walks and tours with all the essential information you need, as well as our pick of where to stay while you are there and select restaurant listings, to complement the more low-key options given in the itineraries.

About the authors

Pocket Rough Guide Italian Lakes Walks & Tours was updated by Ros Belford, building on original content by Susie Boulton and Lisa Gerard-Sharp.

Susie Boulton has travelled extensively in Italy for over 25 years and has written and contributed to many Italian titles. Susie first became acquainted with the Italian Lakes while working for *Holiday Which?* Many of the tours in this book were originally conceived by Italy specialist Lisa Gerard-Sharp.

Help us update

We've gone to a lot of effort to ensure that this edition of the **Pocket Rough Guide Italian Lakes Walks & Tours** is accurate and up-to-date. However, things change – places get "discovered", opening hours are notoriously fickle, restaurants and rooms raise prices or lower standards. If you feel we've got it wrong or left something out, we'd like to know, and if you can remember the address, the price, the hours, the phone number, so much the better.

Please send your comments with the subject line "**Pocket Rough Guide Italian Lakes Walks & Tours Update**" to mail@uk.roughguides.com. We'll acknowledge all contributions and send a copy of the next edition (or any other Rough Guide if you prefer) for the very best emails.

Credits

Pocket Rough Guide Italian Lakes Walks & Tours
Editor: Lizzie Horrocks
Updater: Ros Belford
Author: Susie Boulton, Lisa Gerard-Sharp
Picture Editor: Piotr Kala
Picture Manager: Tom Smyth
Cartography: Berndston & Berndston
Layout: Grzegorz Madejak
Head of DTP and Pre-Press: Rebeka Davies
Head of Publishing: Sarah Clark
Photo credits: 123RF 40/41, 62, 100; Apa Publications 7MR, 17L, 18/19; Dreamstime 21R, 22, 31, 33, 46, 47R, 50/51, 67, 68, 68/69, 83R, 82/83, 84, 120/121, 137; Fotolia 6ML, 23R, 40, 41R, 55L, 60/61, 63, 69R, 84/85; Glyn Genin/Apa Publications 70/71, 72, 72/73, 73R, 101R; Grand Hotel des Iles Borromées 104, 105; Grand Hotel Villa Serbelloni 116/117, 117; iStockphoto 6MC, 7MR, 25, 35, 42, 48, 49R, 48/49, 52, 52/53, 54, 54/55, 64, 66, 82, 86, 124, 125, 128, 130/131; Leonardo 106, 107R, 106/107, 114, 115; Leading Hotels of the World 112T; Mockford & Bonetti/Apa Publications 39R, 46/47, 56, 56/57, 90/91; Neil Buchan-Grant/Apa Publications 6BC, 7T, 7M, 12, 13R, 12/13, 16, 18, 20/21, 22/23, 30, 42/43, 53R, 57R, 58, 59, 60, 65R, 64/65, 78, 80, 81R, 87, 88, 88/89, 89R, 90, 91R, 92, 92/93, 93R, 94, 96, 97, 112, 112/113, 113R, 123, 129, 130, 132, 134, 134/135; Public Domain 6TL, 98/99; Shutterstock 1, 4, 8/9, 10, 11, 14/15, 16/17, 19R, 20, 24, 27T, 28/29, 32, 34, 36/37, 36, 37R, 38, 38/39, 43R, 44/45, 61R, 70, 71R, 74/75, 77, 76, 79, 80/81, 95, 100/101, 107T, 108T, 116L, 119T, 122, 123T, 126/127, 131R, 133, 135R, 136; Terme di Sirmione 85R; Villa D'Este 102/103, 108, 109R, 108/109, 118, 119; Wikimedia Commons/public domain 26, 27
Cover credits: Lake Garda **Shutterstock**

Printed in Czech Republic

This book was produced using **Typefi** automated publishing software.

All Rights Reserved
© 2024 Apa Digital AG
License edition © Apa Publications Ltd UK

First edition 2024

No part of this book may be reproduced, stored in a retrieval system or transmitted in any form or means electronic, mechanical, photocopying, recording or otherwise, without prior written permission from Apa Publications.

Distribution

UK, Ireland and Europe
Apa Publications (UK) Ltd
sales@roughguides.com
United States and Canada
Ingram Publisher Services
ips@ingramcontent.com
Australia and New Zealand
Booktopia
retailer@booktopia.com.au
Worldwide
Apa Publications (UK) Ltd
sales@roughguides.com

Special Sales, Content Licensing and CoPublishing

Rough Guides can be purchased in bulk quantities at discounted prices. We can create special editions, personalised jackets and corporate imprints tailored to your needs.
sales@roughguides.com
http://roughguides.com

INDEX

Index

A

accessible travel 133
Amalfi Coast 66
Angera 35
Arco 96
Argegno 66
Ascona 45
Azienda Agricola Villa wine estate 80

B

Bardolino 87
Baroque period 13
Basilica di San Giulio (Isola di San Giulio) 50
Baveno 40, 44
Belgirate 35
Bellagio 57
Bergamo 70
- Accademia Carrara 70
- Campanone 72
- Cappella Colleoni 72
- Carrara 71
- Cittadella 73
- Duomo 72
- GAMeC 71
- Lower Town 70
- Museo Archeologico 73
- Museo di Scienze Naturali 73
- Museo Donizettiano 72
- Palazzo della Ragione 72
- Piazza del Duomo 72
- Piazza Vecchia 72
- Rocca 73
- Santa Maria Maggiore 72
- Upper Town 71

Bleggio Superiore 97
Boat trips 14
Bornato 81
Borromean Islands 30
Brera 23
Brunate 63
Budgeting 124

C

Cable-car
- Brunate 63

Camedo 47
Camonica Valley 77
Cannero Riviera 44
Cannobio 44
Castello di Arco 96
Castello di Bornato 81
Castello di Drena 96
Castello Oldofredi 74
Castello Scaligero 89
Castel Toblino 96
Centovalli 46
Cernobbio 64
Chiesa dell'Assunta (Orta) 49
Children 124
Cislano 78
Climate 125
Clusane 76
Comano Terme 97
Como Town 60
Corte Franca wine region 81
Culture 10
Cycling 24

D

D'Annunzio, Gabriele 91
Diga Foranea pier 63
Domodossola 47
Driving 132
Duomo (Como Town) 62

E

Emergency numbers 126
Entertainment 22
Erbusco 81

F

Fashion Week 20
Festival of San Giovanni 66
Fiavè 97
Foiling 25
Food and drink 16
Franciacorta wine trail 80

G

Garda 87
Gardone Riviera 87
Gargnano 88
Giardino André Heller 90
Giardino Botanico Alpinia 39
Gignese 48
Golf 25
Grand Hôtel des Iles Borromées 35
Grand Hotel (Gradone Riviera) 90
Grottoes of Catullus 84

H

Health 126
Hiking 24
Hotels
- Albergo Bellavista 110
- Antica Locanda dei Mercanti 113
- Antica Locanda Leonardo 113
- Araba Fenice 110
- Art Hotel 107
- Azienda Agricola 110
- Bellavista 107
- Bologna 107
- Bulgari Hotel 113
- Ca' del Baldo Agriturisimo Relais 111
- Cappucini Convento 110
- Color Hotel 111
- Duomo 112
- Florence 108
- Garden 108
- Gardesena 112
- Gombi Hotel 109
- Grand Hotel 11
- Grand Hotel des Iles Borromées 105
- Grand Hotel Fasano 112
- Grand Hotel Majestic 105
- Grand Hotel Menaggio 108
- Grand Hotel Tremezzo 57, 109
- Grand Hotel Villa Serbelloni 109
- Gran Duca di York 113
- Hotel Aracoeli 106
- Hotel Cortese 106
- Hotel di Varese 107
- Hotel Due Palme 43

Hotel Garni Millenium 105
I Due Roccoli 110
Il Porticciolo 105
Il Sole di Ranco 105
La Bussola 106
L'Albereta 110
Laurin 112
Le Due Corti 108
Leon d'Oro 106
Le Palme 112
Lido 105
Locanda Sant'Anna 109
Locanda San Vigilio 112
Palace Grand Hotel Varese 107
Park Hotel Querceto 113
Petronilla Hotel 109
Piccolo Hotel Olina 106
Pironi 105
Relais Franciacorta 111
Relais Mirabella 110
Relais Villa Porta 104
Riva Lago 110
Villa Aminta 106
Villa Cortine Palace Hotel 113
Villa Crespi 106
Villa d'Este 109
Villa Fiordaliso 113
Villa Gradoni 111

I

Il Vittoriale degli Italiani 91
Intragna 47
Iseo 74
Isola 23
Isola Bella 30
Isola Comacina 66
Isola dei Pescatori 32
Isola del Garda 91
Isola di Loreto 78
Isola di San Giulio 50
Isola Madre 33
Isole Brissago 45

J

James, Henry 11, 32

K

Kitesurfing 25

L

Laglio 65
Lake Como 56, 60, 64
Lake Garda 82, 86, 11
Lake Iseo 74
Lake Lugano 54
Lake Mergozzo 43
Lake Varese 53
La Montina winery 80
language 134
Lavena 54
Lezzeno 66
LGBTQ+ travellers 126
Limone sul Garda 88
Locanda del Isola Comacina 64
Locarno 45
Luino 54

M

Maderno 88
Malcesine 89
markets 20
Markets
Il Mercato di Luino 52
Marone 78
Medieval Gardens 36
Meina 35
Mergozzo 43
Milan 14
Galleria Vittorio Emanuele II 99
La Rinascente 99
La Scala 99
Madonnina 98
Marchesi 1824 99
Museo Poldi Pezzoli 100
Museo Teatrale alla Scala 100
nightlife 101
Pinacoteca di Brera 101
Quadrilatero d'Oro 100
The Brera 100
The Last Supper 100
Zucca 99
Moltrasio 65
money 127
Monte Baldo 89
Monte Isola 75
Monte Mottarone 38
Monticelli Brusati 80
Morcote, Switzerland 55
MTB and eMTB 24
Museo Civico (Rocca) 95
Museo della Bambola (Angera) 36
Museo delle due Guerre (Iseo) 74
Museo dell'Olio di Oliva (Bardolino) 87
Museo dell'Ombrello e del Parasole (Gignese) 48
Museo del Vino (Bardolino) 87
Museo Didattico della Seta 12
Mussolini 93

N

Napoleon 35, 91
Navigli 23
Nesso 66

O

Oratorio di San Giovanni, Isola Comacina 67
Orta San Giulio 49

P

Palazzo Borromeo 31
Pallanza 42
Parco Botanico del Cantone Ticino 45
Parco Nazionale delle Incisioni Rupestri (Ponte) 77
Parco Regionale di Campo dei Fiori 54
Passirano 80
Peschiera Maraglio 75
Pisogne 77
Pognana Lario 66
Ponte Tresa 54
Porta Garibaldi station 23
Porto Ceresio 54
Public holidays 127

R

Ramo di Como 64
Restaurants
Acquadolce 116
Agli Angeli 92
AgriGelateria 51
AgriGelateria 49
Agriturismo del Trenta 120
Albergo Milano 43
Al Boeuc 116
Al Borducan Caffè 55
Al Donizetti 118

Al Pozz 47
Al Sorriso 116
Al Volt 97
Antico Ristorante Boeucc 101
Baretto di San Vigilio 118
Bellavista Hotel & Restaurant 63
Bice 101
Bilacus 59
Bistrot 76 37
Cadebasi 81
Caffe Italia 120
Camin Hotel Colmegna 55
Cantina e Agriturismo Al Rocol 118
Casa delle Neve 39
Cracco 122
Da Franco 118
Da Mimmo 73
El Brellin 122
Esplanade 120
Gatto Moro 120
Gelateria Marghera 123
Grotto Sant'Anna 114
Hostaria Dam a Traa 43
Hotel Bologna 55
Hotel Lido 37
Hotel Ristorante Belvedere 33
Hotel Ristorante Verbano 33
Il Cavatappi 117
Il Gatto Nero 117
Ill Porticciolo 120
Il Maialino di Giò Piazza 73
Il Piccolo Lago 115
Il Sole di Ranco 115
Il Vicoletto 115
Joia 123
La Barchetta 59
La Botte 37
La Citadella 47
La Fiasca 85
Langosteria 123
L'Anima Del Gusto 122
La Quartina 43
La Rucola 121
La Spiaggetta 78
La Terrazza 121
La Tortuga di Orietta 122
La Vineria 120
Leon d'Oro 51
Locanda La Tirlindana 69
Locanda Sant'Anna 117
Lo Scalo 114
Lo Stornello 115
Luini 123
Milano 114
Mistral 117
Olina 51
Osteria al Torcol 85
Osteria Del Centenario 115
Osteria del Gallo 63
Osteria dell'Orologio 92
Osteria di Mezzo 92
Osteria Santo Cielo 89
Pasticceria Cova 101
Pasticceria Vassalli 120
Piccolo Mondo 97
Punta dell'Est 118
Relais I due Roccoli 119
Relais Mirabella 119
Restel de Fer 121
Risorgimento 121
Ristorante/Bar Funicolare 47
Ristorante Castel 121
Ristorante Il Vicoletto 115
Ristorante LeoneFelice 119
Ristorante Re Lear 121
Roof Garden 119
Silvio 59
Sociale 63
Teatro 117
Trattoria al Porto 81
Trattoria del Gallo 81
Trattoria del Muliner 119
Trattoria Santo Stefano 69
Trattoria Vecchia Malcesine 89
Vecchia Riva 116
Vecchia Varenna 117
Villa Aminta 115
Villa Crespi 116
Villa d'Este 118
Villa Feltrinelli 122
Villa Fiordaliso 122
Vineria Cozzi 73
Riserva Naturale Fondotoce 42
Riserva Naturale Piramidi di Zone 78
Riserva Naturale Torbiere del Sebino 80
Riva del Garda 88
Riva di Solto 76
Rocca Borromeo 35
Rocca Scaligera (Sirmione) 82
rock-climbing 25

S

Sacro Monte di Varese 54
Sacro Monte (Orta) 48
Sailing 24, 25
Salò 88, 93
San Carlone statue 36
San Fedele basilica (Como Town) 62
San Giovanni 59
San Pietro in Lamosa (Iseo) 80
San Pietro (Sirmione) 84
Santa Anna della Rocca (Sirmione) 83
Santa Caterina del Sasso 39
Santa Maria della Neve (Pisogne) 78
Santa Maria in Valvendra (Lovere) 77
Santa Maria Maggiore 47
Santa Maria Maggiore (Sirmione) 83
Santuario della Madonna del Sasso 46, 51
Santuario Madonna della Ceriola (Monte Isola) 75
Sarnico 76, 81
Settimane Musicali 22
shopping 20
Silk 21, 12
Sirmione 82, 86
Skiing 25
Stresa 34
Suna 42
Surfing 25

T

Telephones 128
Tempio Voltiano (Como Town) 62
Tenno 97
Terme di Sirmione 83
Torbole 96
Torno 65
Torri del Benaco 88
Toscolano 88
Tourist information 128
Tours and guides 129
Transport 129
Tremezzo 57
Trentino 94

V

Varese 52
Villa Carlotta 56
Villa Cicogna-Mozzoni 55
Villa Clara at Baveno 11
Villa Crespi 51
Villa del Balbianello 12, 68
Villa d'Este 66
Villa Giulia 42
Villa Melzi 58
Villa Olmo (Brunate) 63
Villa Pallavicino 35
Villa Panza 52
Villa Pliniana 65
Villa Serbelloni 58
Villa Taranto 40
Visas and passports 133

W

Watersports 24

Z

Zone 78

MAP LEGEND

Start of tour
Tour & route direction
Recommended sight
Recommended restaurant/café
Place of interest
Tourist information
Statue/monument
Main post office
Main bus station
Metro station
Cable car
Villa
Park
Important building
Hotel
Transport hub
Shop / market
Pedestrian area
Urban area